THE BEAST IN THE BEAUTY

AN INSIDE LOOK AT THE WORLD OF BEAUTY FROM CHALLENGES TO SUCCESS

A BOOK COLLABORATION WITH INTERNATIONALLY RENOWN STYLISTS AND ARTISTS IN THE BEAUTY INDUSTRY

Kevin KIRK
INTERNATIONAL AWARD-WINNING STYLIST

Vicki KIRK MAY
INTERNATIONAL AWARD-WINNING AUTHOR

Jai Publishing
WRITE. RELEASE. HEAL.

Jai Publishing House Incorporated
info@jaipublishing.com
www.jaipublishing.com

Scripture quotations marked (NLT) are taken from the Holy Bible, New Living Translation, copyright ©1996, 2004, 2015 by Tyndale House Foundation. Used by permission of Tyndale House Publishers, a Division of Tyndale House Ministries, Carol Stream, Illinois 60188. All rights reserved.

Cover art by Chrissi Knighton Burrell, www.thedesignbrand.com

Printed in the United States of America

Hardcover ISBN-13: 978-1-7352082-1-3
Paperback ISBN: 978-1-7352082-2-0

Other Works by Vicki Kirk May

✦ The Whole Truth & Nothing But The Truth, So Help Me Teachers! (Award-winning book)

✦ The Evolution of an Educator (#1 Bestselling book)

Both are available now on Amazon

Table of Contents

Foreword

by Dr. Mike McClure, Sr.

☀ ☀ ☀

I've known Kevin Kirk for the greater part of 20 years, and I believe the entire time I've known Kevin, he has always maintained a deep desire and dream of making a powerful, yet positive, impact within and upon the Beauty Industry.

BEAUTY is defined as the quality present in a thing or person that gives intense pleasure or deep satisfaction to the mind, whether arising from sensory manifestations (shape, color, sound, etc.), a meaningful design or pattern, or something else (as a personality in which high spiritual qualities are manifest).

The BEAST in these writings represent those obstacles and challenges that tend to oppose the hopes and dreams of forward thinkers that dare to see the wonderful possibilities that for too long lay dormant beneath the masterpiece of minimalism.

In this book, Kevin confronts the harsh reality that there is stiff competition in the industry and inner challenges in the individual that must be overcome to achieve success.

Through this practical list of thoughts, tools, and tips, Kevin equips and emancipates the reader to fulfill their dreams, desires, and destiny.

The serious dreamer must make this book a regular resource in their journey towards success.

The BEAST in the BEAUTY

Book Collaboration with Experts
in the Beauty Industry

Lead by: Kevin Kirk & Vicki Kirk May

style 1

The Beast in The Beauty Interview with Kevin Kirk

by Kevin Kirk

To watch the LIVE taping of the Behind the Scenes Interview, go to **bit.ly/beastinthebeauty**
Password Required: beast2020 (case sensitive)

Kevin Kirk gathered five other hair stylists who all work in the same industry, yet have different backgrounds, upbringings, economic status, etc. He wanted to showcase one topic from different points of view, and he succeeded with his selection—a diverse set of hair stylists. The stylists were eager to share their story as how often are hair stylists really asked to tell the "other" side of the story, you know, the not-so-glitzy and not-so-glamorous side?

The conversation was taped live at a non-disclosed location. What you will read will be the true and authentic hearts of hair stylists who have endured trials and challenges in and outside of the salon. These stylists also compete in one of the largest hair show competitions in the world, but their journey to getting to that stage has not been an easy one.

When asked why write this book, the answer was quite simple for Kevin:

> *"We want to expose people to the challenges and the struggles that we have doing what we do [in the beauty industry]. A lot of times, from the outside looking in, it looks like we're just partying, having fun while doing hair and making a lot of money. But this beauty industry has a lot of different challenges—physically, mentally, spiritually, and, I think most of all, emotionally.*
>
> *What I wanted to do was get in the room with like-minded hairstylists, all of us in different points of our careers, and have an honest conversation about our personal challenges within this industry as well as the things that inspire us.*
>
> *Even though this lifestyle comes with many challenges, and even some situations you will find yourself crying, there's still something about this industry, and something that's in us [the stylists], that makes us keep getting up and going back and putting our heart out there."*

Continue reading for an abbreviated transcription of that conversation below.

To watch the LIVE taping of the Behind the Scenes Interview, go to **bit.ly/beastinthebeauty**
Password Required: beast2020 (case sensitive)

Let's get started! Each stylist answered two main questions: (1) What is your "Beast", meaning that thing(s) that challenges/ challenged you, and (2) What is your "Beauty", meaning that thing(s) that inspires you. Here's what they said…

Stylist 1: Kevin Kirk

THE BEAST: I will say that one of my biggest struggles is the fear of failure. The beast for me is continuing to maintain that high level of success. You would think it gets easier, but the more you win [any competition], or the more you accomplish a milestone, the bigger your name becomes, the bigger the challenges—it is the cost of fame. So, in my opinion, being successful in the beauty industry can be quite challenging.

The weight that an influencer carries come from the fans. An influencer understands that if they don't show up, they disappoint the very people who support them. They have something to lose. In the beginning of my career, I was fearless, you know, I didn't have anything to lose per se. So I took more risks, because I wasn't in my head about being famous.

Don't get me wrong. I was building a name for myself—I had won a couple of hair shows, made the cover of some major magazines, and leading two dynamic styling teams. People actually looked up to me at that point. The pressure of fame made me feel like every little mistake felt ten times worse! What I do affects not only me, but my fans... my supporters.

Then, on the aspect of me being a father and a husband, I want my family to look up to me. But even more than that, I have to provide for them. One of the biggest life lessons that I've experienced in doing hair was actually the end of the culmination of one of my greatest accomplishments.

❦

It was 2005—the first time I won Bronner Brothers, and that was a challenge within itself! I will start off by saying that I didn't *come* from money. I mean, we grew up emotionally and spiritually rich, but financially poor. Well, let me tell the whole story...

Before I was even invited to be a part of Bronner Brothers, I was nominated for Cutter of the Year at a hair show in Washington D.C. I think it was called "the Golden Shears" at the time; I didn't think I would win, but the nomination was enough for me to go.

I didn't have enough money to make the trip alone, so I partnered with a friend to split the costs. I bought my airline tickets, reserved my hotel room, and then I got the news... my business partner told me that she couldn't go after all! I thought, *"Man what am I going to do? How am I going to pay for everything? I couldn't really afford to do this trip without her, I was counting on her to pay her half of the costs, then she bailed out on me. What am I going to do?"*

I will be in Washington D.C. for the entire weekend, and I only have $200... that's it...$200. I was faced with the decision—either I am going to bail out or I am going to go to D.C. and try to live off of $200 for a weekend? Me being who I am, I flew my butt out to D.C. on a budget of $200 and a plan.

Then another friend called and said, "Kevin, I'm in town, but I just got robbed. I don't have anywhere else to stay. My models won't have anywhere to stay and I'm out of money." This was a good friend of mine, so I said, "Okay, you and your team can stay in my room." I gave him $100 of the $200 budget, which left me with only $100. I budgeted everything, even down to what I ate. I would order two cheeseburgers and a cup of water for only $1.50. I had a plan and I worked that plan!

❦

Once I arrived in D.C. and checked in the hotel, as I'm walking through the lobby of the hotel where the show was hosted, I ran into Jerry Dingle—the Vice President of

Bronner Brothers at the time. Jerry Dingle would never remember my name. He'd come to the salon, look at me (trying to remember my name) and say, "Hey you." Every time I would see Jerry, I had to reintroduce myself. Every time!

However, this particular time, Jerry saw me in the crowd, walked up to me and said, "Hey Kevin, how are you doing?" Blew my mind! *Wow, Mr. Dingle remembered me!* He asked, "You want to get something to eat and drink?" Of course I said, "Let's do that." Keeping my cool.

We went to the hotel bar, ordered food and drinks and just talked. The whole time we were talking, I was thinking, "*What is protocol? Do I pay for all of this?*" The bill was getting higher and higher as we ordered more food and drinks. I could barely enjoy the conversation because I was trying to add up how much all of this was going to cost. I had two drinks and they had two appetizers. I thought, "*God, I don't think my card is going to hold. This is going to be so embarrassing.*"

The conversation continues. I try to take my mind off of that bill. I had the opportunity to tell the Vice President of Bronner Brothers my dreams and goals in the industry. He shared with me how the industry was evolving and how to be prepared for the evolution. Then, out of the blue, Jerry said, "You know what, Kevin, I can't make any promises, but we are one contestant short in Houston. If you submit [your application], I'll make sure your name get to the top of the list. It's not my decision, but I'm gonna make sure that your name at least get looked at." Astonished and excited, I responded, "Okay, sir, I will submit [the application] now."

What no one knew at that time was that I had never competed in a hair show before. I had showcased a lot, but I had never competed on that [Bronner Brothers] level. It really was just like a showcase, but who turns down the opportunity to perform or compete at Bronner Brothers? AND the cash prize was $10,000!

❦

Now, back to that dinner with drinks bill… when the waiter brought the bill over and placed it on the table, I reached for it, but Jerry stopped me and said, "No, I got this." You have no idea how relieved I was when he grabbed that bill! But again, I didn't know protocol at that time because I was new to everything, so really the protocol, he was *supposed* to pay for it.

At any rate, as I promised Jerry at the dinner, I submitted my application for the competition in Houston and I was accepted! I was on my way to Bronner Brothers to compete in Houston for the competition. I couldn't afford to rent a car, and I had to drive 13 miles from my home to the competition, but my wife and I had a minivan. I reserved two hotel rooms, but we had a married couple with us. The married couple took one room and the rest of us stayed in the other room. We were all piled up in that one room— three of us were sleeping on the couch. We were all on top of each other, packed tight, but man, I was probably at the height of my cutting game at that time. I was putting everything I had out there for this career. I took chances and leaned into every opportunity and door that was opened to me.

In Houston, we had 15 minutes to perform. We didn't have a huge budget or anything; our costume was cut-up jeans and t-shirts. That was it. And in that 15 minutes, I performed seven haircuts! Now if you ask me if I can do that today, my answer would be *heck no*! (LOL) But at that moment, I was like Edward Scissorhands—I was just in the zone, and they were good haircuts, too! We blew everybody away.

The other contestants spent money on props and costumes, and they had intricate dance routines. We didn't have any of that; but at the end of the night, they were so mad at me that I couldn't leave! Seriously, security came to me and my team and told us, "You all have to wait here because there's a group of people out there waiting to beat you up!" Some of the other contestants, their models and their friends were rioting outside, thus security wouldn't let us leave for our own safety. It was crazy, but we won!

That win qualified me to go on to Baltimore, where we won again. That's why I say that your Intro for the show has to be something that's heartfelt...that grabs the audience. In my Intro, I started off saying, "They said I didn't deserve to be here..." I was making reference to that little incident in Houston, where they tried to downplay my victory by saying I really didn't "win".

I went through a whole lot as I was building a brand in this industry. I faced a lot of criticisms—how I was the underdog and how people felt like, not only I shouldn't win, but that I didn't even deserve to be in the place. That was hurtful, you know. So in my Intro in Baltimore, I laid it all out on that stage. I gave my all because, to me, when you have nothing to lose, you don't keep everything. Don't hold anything back.

I tell you this, I would rather walk away and find a loss that I felt good about and that I gave it my all, than to look back with regrets of what I should've or could've done. So I put all of my heart and passion and dreams out there on that stage. As a result, and in only one month, we won in two different states— $60,000 prize.

🌱

Bronner Brothers invited me to teach a class on hair coloring that actually turned into a whole tour of scheduled classes. I was teaching hair coloring, cutting… I was making a name for myself. I was getting a lot of love from everywhere, except my home city. My home city was like, "Oh that's just Kevin." But I'd [still] do a hair show there. I've been doing a hair show in Birmingham for a considerable period of time that's been extremely successful.

Overall, I've always had a good support system. There was this one particular time I was preparing for another hair show. A couple of months prior to the show, I was in a horrible car accident that left me trapped inside the car. My left hand was paralyzed for a while and I couldn't work. To this day, there's a scar right here on my hand from being stuck under the steering wheel. I was devastated!

That was life changing because that's when I really saw just how volatile... how easy you can be on top of the world one moment, then hit rock bottom in the blink of an eye! I couldn't do hair anymore because my left hand was injured. As a result, I lost half of my clientele, and no one came out to support my hair show.

I came under the fire from my own hometown. They accused me of being arrogant and cocky because I had won a couple of Bronner Brothers hair show competitions... I had zero support, lost all of the money I had, I couldn't pay my bills, I couldn't work—it was one of the toughest conversations I ever had to have with my wife.

I remember that day so vividly because she [my wife] was washing dishes, cooking and cleaning up, and I had to tell her that we were about to lose our home. Talk about the worst feeling for a man. We had three kids, and I couldn't provide for them, I couldn't keep the house, I couldn't provide for my wife. So I'm really feeling like I was nothing. I felt defeated.

I'm so thankful for my pastor. One Sunday, there was a men's conference and something was said that moved me. I walked out of the conference room and went upstairs to the classroom in which I used to teach Sunday School. I kneeled down and prayed with everything I had within me. And I just surrendered everything to God, so much so that when I rose upon my feet, I didn't feel defeated anymore. I knew in that very moment that whatever I was going through, it wasn't bigger than God.

My faith just went to another level because from that point, all I was doing was confessing His Word over my life… I wasn't going to feel defeated, I wasn't going to be less than a man. That was the last lesson I learned on that, because prior to that I felt like a man was somewhat defined by the money, on the income that he made because he was the provider.

But then I realized that we (men) provide more, or should provide more, than only finances. We should be spiritual and emotional leaders. I mean, there's so many different things to be in a family than just give them money. I, as a man, have value. I'm still the head of my household; I'm still the man; I'm still going to do for my family. When you take a problem to God, leave it. And that's what I did.

It's no longer about me. All I have to do is be willing to walk the right path, and have the courage to follow the path that He gives me. It's up to Him to provide. So I took that pressure off of me and I put it on Him [God}. And man, it's been a battle. Most people have no idea of the struggles [I've had]. What I love about God is that no one knew. No one saw it from the outside of what was going on inside of me, until that day I prayed.

Through that stretch though, even though we were still in our home, the utilities were shut off. There's nothing like being in a cold house with your kids, and you can't turn the heater on.

That's why I tell people now, you have to have the faith and the courage to walk out your purpose, no matter how hard it gets. Don't let your fear stop you. Because if I allowed my fear to stop me, I wouldn't be where I am right now. It's a blessing to be a blessing to you.

That's why push you all [my team] the way I do because fear cannot stop us. The lack of resources... it's not an excuse. You can do anything you set your mind to.

Look at it like this: none of us here in this room came from a whole lot of money. We grew up poor. All of us. But look at us now—which proves my point that money is not the *only* resource. It's just the only one that people talk about.

But all I had then and have now is God. All I have is my faith in Him. All I have is His Word. And I'll tell you right now, His Word is way more powerful than money will ever be. Money will fail you. Money gives you a false sense of confidence. God never will.

So that was my beast. That was the thing that I had to overcome. That was my challenge.

☀

THE BEAUTY: My beauty is what I'm doing right now. It's sharing my life, my experience, my knowledge, my information, and helping people that are in similar situations. I may not know the intimate details, but I know they have dreams and goals, but they don't necessarily have the money or the resources to finance them. I've been there, so I definitely know how to help them where they are.

You will notice that when I'm backstage, I'm always talking about how to make more money… making a better life for your family, making a better life for your kids, leaving a legacy.

It's not because I love money, it's because of what I've been through. I could've given up, but I didn't. I could've allowed fear to stop me, but I didn't and everyday that challenge is still with me. You think I don't remember that feeling? I remember it, but I keep on pushing. And I don't want people to go through what they're going through then give up before their breakthrough.

❦

I keep on pushing the beauty. The beauty of it is I got that fearlessness back in my life again. Not because I'm making so much more money, but because of my faith in God. I'm not relying on the money. I'm relying on Him and I know He's not going to leave me. And the most beautiful part of it is that I see myself inspiring others to do the same.

Stylist 2: Miranda

THE BEAST: One piece of my beast was being respected by my peers in the industry.

Growing up, I was raised to be an engineer. Everything I studied while in school was engineering and chemistry. So regardless, I was raised to go to college. My siblings, my parents, all of them are college graduates. This is just what we do. And I was happy about it. You know, I went on all the college tours. I enjoyed life. I've met a lot of people in all of the programs outside of school, but I loved hair.

Since I can remember, I was always playing in hair. I had a gift of a three foot doll that was like a "My Size" Barbie. I went out on my grandparents' porch the very next day after getting it and I cut all of her hair off! My mom said, "What are you doing?" It was a short cut because I had twin aunts who always had the baddest short haircuts. And I said, "Look, she's a triplet. She's part of the family now!"

I always loved doing hair to the point where my hairstylist used to let me do their hair. They would always teach me. But I just thought it was something to do for fun on the side. When I was in the ninth or 10th grade, I remember being told about the vocational program, one of which was cosmetology. Of course, I wanted to go but I had to convince my mom first. I approached my mom with a plan and said, "Mom, if I promise you that I would still go to college, can I go to hair school?"

At the time, I was doing everyone's hair, I was the braider in the city; so I was already making money. My plan was to use that to pay for hair school. After showing my mom the cost of the school and how I could pay for it myself, she agreed and I was in! I held up my part of the bargain and I worked my butt off in school. I made the Principal's list in the first quarter.

I still had my engineering and chemistry programs out-of-school, but I kept up with all of my studies. I actually ended up graduating with double honors. I also had the highest score out of two cosmetology schools on exam the day we went to State board, and granted me access to scholarship money.

❧

I love my family and our bond is unbreakable. It's weird though because it kinda didn't prepare me for the real world. I learned the hard way that not everyone has a supportive family like I did, that would cause them to do some not-so-cool things.

The backstory is: I had become close with this individual to the point where when I was in need, she really came through for me. So I trusted her enough to move around to different salons, following her. When she moved, I moved. We moved to four different salons. This last location, we shared overhead expenses, and I paid her my share while she paid the owner. At the time, it was a great business deal. I knew exactly what I was paying for, and the numbers fit my budget. Everything was going good. We moved in our salon in February, and the following August, my friend / business partner called me one day and said she needed to meet with me.

We met at the salon and she told me that she was being evicted in 30 days. She told me the building manager said they had a waiting list, but we should go talk to him and see if I could get the space (I wanted my own space anyway). When we arrived to the building manager's office, he said, "You don't have 30 days, you have until the weekend."

My heart dropped to my stomach! But before we left, the manager told my friend, if I was to sign the lease, I could stay, but she [my friend] still owed the money. To me, that was still good news because at least the eviction wouldn't go on her record.

I spent the weekend stressing out trying to figure out if this was the move I needed to make. And, of course, I prayed all weekend. That's all I could do. By Monday morning, I decided to sign the lease for two years. Immediately, I started making changes to the space; I bought at least $500 worth of equipment and things from my friend. The issue arose when it was time for me to share with her how I wanted to run the salon—as the new owner.

Trouble struck our relationship in a major way. I called Kevin, and other salon owners, asking them for business advice on how to run a salon. I didn't mean for it to be offensive, but at the end of the day, if you [my friend] messed up so badly that you lost the shop, and I'd seen you do all of this right in front of me, then you're not the person I'm going to for business advice. There's hair talent, and then there's business, and she wasn't good at the business side of things. That was the problem. It ended up hurting our friendship because she wasn't taking care of the business.

It's just business, but people can't separate business and friendship. So they ended up intertwining the two and messing up something good. I liked the relationships I had, but at the end of the day, if you don't respect me and my business, it's going to be a problem... and THAT is a beast!

Long story short, she ended up leaving the salon without notice, breaking the contract and taking another stylist with her. I felt disrespected and hurt. That is really my beast, being hurt by a good friend in the same industry.

....

Watch Miranda's full story on *The Beast in the Beauty* documentary: bit.ly/beastinthebeauty. Use password (case sensitive): beast2020

....

☀

THE BEAUTY: One of my beauty is the connections that I've made and being able to help others. I love doing hair and the beauty is my clients are wonderful! I get to have a connection with so many people—lawyers, doctors, some are even millionaires. They come in, they relax, they unwind… they're committed to me, and I'm committed to them.

Stylist 3: Rickeshia "Ricki" Cole

THE BEAST: My beast was really trying to find out who I was as a person. Coming out of high school, I was one of the few in my class that graduated that didn't know what I wanted to do after high school. I did hair in school, but it wasn't like a thing that I was gonna make a career out of it. It was more like something to do right now.

I was always a hard worker. I had a job since I was 13 years old [babysitting]. And then I moved to work at the mall. Though I always liked the money coming in, still I kept thinking that I have to find something that I really like.

College just wasn't for me. We went on many college tours, I saw the fraternity life and all of that, and I knew then and there that I didn't like that life.

Well, one day my aunt came over to the house for me to do her hair. She said, "You need to get serious about this and stop this kitchen beautician stuff. Get legit. You're really good at what you do. Put your name on it and run with it."

I enrolled in school and, at the time, I was still living with my parents, but they were going through a divorce. I felt like my father dropped the ball when it came to his family. He left us, and my mom couldn't handle the finances on her own, so we lost our house.

I moved in with a friend and still went to school; then one day I decided to use the money I was getting from school to go out and get a place of my own. I had no idea what that meant as far as being on my own, like the basic thing of getting from one place to another place. I didn't have a car so I was asking friends for a ride or I'm taking public transportation (the bus) to school and work.

By this time, I was working part-time at Burlington Coat Factory and I hated it. And then I was going to school full time, so that transition of trying to figure out how I was going to do hair and make some money while out here in the real world was challenging. But God definitely provided for me.

❦

Becoming a legit hairstylist became my focus. I began the work to build clientele. I went to colleges to the Greek parties—where a lot of my clientele came from at first. Then I also got involved with fashion shows in my area. I would volunteer my services to the models… from which again I gained a lot of clients.

Now, once I built up my clientele, I lived smack dab in the middle of the hood, so a lot of them didn't want to come there. But at the same time, it was really good for me because it was affordable.

Two years in the game now, but all of my clients were college students so when they went away for the summer, I was back at square one again. That's when I realized that I needed to take this career to another level. So then I started trying to change my clientele… How was I going to get more people who were not students? I started doing my pastor's wife hair, and she would tell her coworkers and then my clientele started to change that way.

When I had a new clientele, it was time to change my living area next. My new clients weren't comfortable coming to where I worked because of the bad area, so I had to move to a more comfortable spot—which also meant I had to spend more money because it costs to go to where you need to be.

My new suite that I worked out of was $100 a week. I said, "Okay, Lord, if this is for me, it's going to be a spot right there for me. I know that You're going to set it up." And He [God] did! He set it up, and I paid that $100 a week, but baby, I ate noodles for a good six months until I got the flow of how to keep the money going!

Money management was another beast for me because I did not get that training growing up—how to manage money, how to save, how to put what you need away and make it work.

❦

Another beast that scared me was boredom. I am a very hands on type of learner, and I like to do different things. But I became bored in this industry and I was only three years in!

I didn't tell my family because when I first told them that I was going to do hair, they said, "Okay, well what's your real job going to be?" That was a slap in the face—I really liked what I did and they just, to me, didn't think that it was up to par.

I had cousins who had aspirations of becoming brain surgeons or professional athletes, and then there was me… who was just the hairstylist, you know, so I have to make this work. My family's response was what really put fire under me to pursue this career with everything I had.

And when I grew bored, that scared me because I've been telling people that I was going to make it. I went to my first hair show in 2014, the Texas International Hair Show. I observed the show, the floor, and the competitions, and I was so inspired. A new fire was lit and I found what I wanted to do!

My first hair competition was in my home town. I was nervous because I'd never competed before and here I was competing against 20 contestants. I was number 16 of the

20 contestants; and these other contestants had 10-20 models, people flipping upside down, flipping back and forth and bullet holes... I mean it was just a whole theatrical backstage. And all I had were three models. Tammie was my mentor and she taught me what to do from point A to point B. My theme was fire and our song was *This Girl is On Fire* by Alicia Keys. And we won first place—$3,000 grand prize!

We walked out of there as the winner and Tammie pulled me to the side and said, "You got something." That was the first time somebody ever told me that, other than my mom who has always been a big supporter. And from that point on, I knew what I wanted to do with my life.

I went on to Bronner Brothers, met Kevin and the rest is history.

☀

THE BEAUTY: Once I found myself, I discovered my passion, my fire for doing hair. My home town is starting to look up to me now, so I don't want to let them down. At the same time, I feel like I'm on the right path, I have the right people around me and I have the right mentors to look up to. I'm so inspired and it's just, you know, beautiful to see Black people doing what we do. So I'm excited.

Stylist 4: Jammie B

THE BEAST: Okay, well I actually have a few beasts, because I do so many different things in the industry. I distribute KirkPro products. I visit different salons to talk to the hairstylists. I am also a hairstylist and work behind the chair during the week when I am not working BabylissPro. And then for BabylissPro, I'm an educator and platform artist where we do hair shows.

But I just see so many different things in the industry going on that I wish we could change so that we all could do better. If I could come up with one word, that word would be commitment. I don't feel like we as the beauty experts are committed. We have great ideas, but then we all have these fears that hold us back.

I'm originally from Jackson, Mississippi and I have been in the beauty industry for 11 years. I went to college, but didn't know what I wanted to do. But when I moved to Birmingham, Alabama, I had been married for 15 years.

Shortly after I moved, I met Bernard, which lead me to Kevin and everyone else. And before that, honestly, I didn't know what I wanted to do with my career. Being around you all, I started modeling and it helped me to see that hair was it for me. When I started cosmetology school, I realized that I went to school to be a teacher.

And then I saw Kevin, he was competing and I thought, *Ooh, I can perform, I can compete...* I could do make-up if I wanted to, I could have my own salon. There were so many different things I could do. It was when I started working with Kevin that helped me realize what I really want to do.

❦

But back up for a second, before all of that, bullsh*t hit me walking right into that—I was married for 15 years and my husband was up for a job for promotion, but we had to relocate. I loved where I was and I was just getting started with the industry.

I told him that I wanted to go to [cosmetology] school, and I needed to know if we were going relocate or stay. He said, "You just finish school and come later." But I'm pretty sure in his mind, he was thinking he was gone.

And so I stayed and finished school. Through that process, we talked on the phone; and eventually before I finished cosmetology school, we were getting ready to get a divorce. Wow. Yeah. What happened? Well, we had problems before that honestly. We just grew apart.

I got married at an early age, I was 22 years old and, I'll be honest, I didn't get married because I wanted to. I got married to make people happy. But I mean, I made the best of it. It was a good marriage. Honestly, we learned a lot, you know. However we ended up getting a divorce, and it was very scary for me because I had never lived alone.

To paint a picture for you: I was in cosmetology school, lived in a house by myself. My ex-husband took everything with him so I had no furniture. I had a mattress on the floor, a TV and my clothes. I was starting a new career, and y'all, what about money? Money was a struggle because I was always afraid of whether I was going to be able to make it on my own. I've never been on my own, so I was doing whatever I had to do, worked different jobs, and one of them was being an exotic dancer.

I danced for seven years and I paid for cosmetology school with money from dancing.

That was my struggle. Having to go through that divorce and going through different phases of my life of learning who I was, what I liked, what I didn't like, what I needed. Just getting to know who I was and to be honest with you, I still struggle with a lot of those issues now because being in the industry, as a leader, you're performing in front of people and, unfortunately, people can be very judgmental. It's hurtful.

Well, I just recently had a full hysterectomy. But it's been years of having to go under the knife for different issues. When it came to my body, the first thing was I had to have back surgery. And two years later, I had to have double knee surgery. While this was going on, I was having fibroid issues and ended up having to get my fibroids removed the next year after I had my knee surgery, during which they found cells that could form into this new type of a rare cancer that didn't respond to chemo. The full hysterectomy now put me at risk of being able to conceive. That really hurt because

I've always wanted kids, and now I can't have them. It's just me now. No family. No husband. Just me and my work.

☀

THE BEAUTY: My beauty is reaching that *one*. It's being able to help others, that is the thing that keeps me going. For one, I always wondered what my purpose was, and I realized it is to help people in any way I can; it may not always be money, it can just be a word of encouragement… and that's my beauty… the people that I meet, the people that support me. I know that there are some people that I can call, like all of you here, and you, Kevin. I know that I have grown a whole lot, and I am where I am now [in my career] because of you [Kevin].

Stylist 5: Ajua Mason

THE BEAST: As far as having beasts in my life, most of the things we deal with in our adulthood stems from our childhood. And you may not exactly realize the moment when it happens or the root from where it came from, but oftentimes it carries on into your adulthood.

And for me, I've dealt with self-worth and lack of value, and also putting other people's needs and wants before my own. And putting other people's opinions, too, before my own was one of my biggest challenges—there's a title for that: people pleaser.

Like I said, I don't know how I got so deeply rooted in it, but it probably has to do with my father who pretty much abandoned me and my mom. I was only a year old, so of course my mom told me this story: my dad was a taxi driver and at the time we lived in Tulsa. My dad didn't like Tulsa, he said it was too slow, so he decided to move to St. Petersburg, Florida.

The plan was for me and my mom to move to Mississippi, and my father would eventually send for us once he got everything situated. I'm not sure how much time passed by, but obviously we didn't move to Florida. I don't know the meat and potatoes behind that story, only that I didn't grow up around my dad.

I really don't have many memories of him either, except for years later when he was about to be deported to Africa and he wanted my mom to come to New York to prove that they were still married and he could stay in the States. She [my mom] agreed to do that mostly because she knew that one day, I would want to have a relationship with him. I was four years old at that time.

So from 1 to 4 years old, I didn't see my dad until she agreed to go to New York to help him. After they had gotten all of the paperwork situated, I remember my mom saying to me, "Look at your daddy because this may be the last time you see him."

Well, that actually was the last time I would physically see my dad.

After New York, we went our separate ways. He moved by to St. Petersburg, me and my mom went back to Mississippi, then later on to Texas. So when I was about 10 years old, my dad had found us in Texas and that's when I found out he was sick and had been trying to find us.

He was on dialysis and stuff like that, and that time he was only 46. So we began having phone communications, but this was in 1995 so long distance was something that like only rich people had. I'll never forget, me and my mom would go to the corner store, get a calling card, go to the pay phone and call him. And that was my interaction. That's how I was able to keep in contact with him. And you know, I remember the sound of his voice, things like that.

My dad was telling me some things that he was doing. He was big into inventing stuff. He sent me a little bit of money here and there, you know, I could tell he was really trying to get to know me and then, eventually he just passed away.

So I never got to go there to see him, we didn't even go to the funeral. Again, I was 10 at that time. So I guess just not having that father figure, not knowing what it's like to have a father, I'm sure that might've affected my personality.

Some people turn to bitterness and anger, you know, it really just depends on the road you decided to take. The road I decided to take was, and I figured it out, it was the lack of self-worth.

I wondered, "Why do I not feel worthy?" and it came to me… I felt like I blamed myself for my father not being in my life. You know, why? Because I felt like I wasn't worthy enough to have him in my life. Like I didn't deserve it. I'm not worthy enough to know him as my father. So that began the whole lack of self-worth.

And eventually when I became an adult and started a career in hairdressing, that [feeling] trickled down into my career. So in the sense of my career, the beast in that is when I deal with my clients, the whole lack of self-worth, the value and all this and that. It's hard for me to charge what I'm really worth, cause if I raise my prices, they won't come to me. They'll go somewhere else. They'll leave me. Just like my father left me. They'll abandoned me just like my father abandoned me.

So that's kind of like the connection that I was able to make. So it's like, no, I gotta do whatever it takes to keep this person in my life, to keep them happy, to keep them wanting to be around me because that's what causes me to have that sense of worth—it is through other people wanting to be in my life.

That's kind of my beast that I'm still overcoming, you know, every day is a struggle and things like that.

☼

THE BEAUTY: The beauty will be: I think the Lord has just always had my back. I think He's always been able to just place opportunities in front of me. I am a go-getter, so I do have the drive, I'm able to present myself, to put myself in these situations to have the opportunity. But ultimately it is God who grants me the opportunity...

Like [for example] the opportunity to be on the Babyliss team. Nowadays I look around and there's hundreds, if not thousands, of people that want this opportunity at this point in 2020, but 10 years ago it was like, God just kind of placed it in my lap, you know what I mean? I didn't really have to do all of this fighting for it like everybody is doing now. So I just feel like, you know, God, He shows Himself to me in different ways, basically saying, "See, I'm your Father. I still have your back. I'm with you."

Stylist 6: Christina "KiKi" Rose

THE BEAST: Yeah, I can say that I related with everybody's story, and their struggles and everything. I would say probably my biggest beast in this industry and in life is overcoming my shyness, which a lot of people don't really believe me when I admit how truly shy I am. Like even right now [sitting here with y'all], there's social anxiety when it comes to the personal level. So people don't usually believe me because on the professional level, I have more confidence because I know what I know and I'm only gonna offer what I know.

So I'm OK with that. My dad always taught me to do it right the first time or don't do it at all. And that's carried me through my professional life ever since I was 15 years old and started working.

I've always worked a job, done it to the best of my ability. Excelled, moved up quickly, and been fine, but socially I'm petrified. I have severe social anxiety. I love people, but I don't. I'm the quiet one. I'm the one that sits back. I'm good listening. I'm not the one that likes to be on the spot… like now, like this gives me the most anxiety because when Kevin asked me to do this [interview]. I was literally like, "Are you sure?" I said I would do it but I've been stressed about it since then, but I'm not good at talking about myself, and I don't know why.

I don't know… probably because I was the youngest child and I was used to just being [in the background]. I like learning from my brother and sister. My sister was very aggressive, kind of that Type A out there personality. My mom always said that like looking back at our childhood, I was always the quiet one, like sitting back.

> {Kevin}: I have noticed that about you. But I think, in my opinion, that's one of your strongest assets.

KiKi: Well, I never looked at it as an asset. Hmmm

{Kevin}: You are a good friend and to your friends, I bet you're their biggest cheerleader and supporter and you help more people than you will ever know. You know? I do believe that.

Sometimes that Type A personality, that aggressive personality, it would look like, man, I wish I could have some of that. But you know, nine times out of 10, that person in the front couldn't be in the front if it wasn't for a person like you [Kiki]. Yeah, I mean, when it's all said and done. So you're saying your shyness has been your biggest struggle, do you think it has hindered you?

Kiki: Well, I feel like it's been something that I've constantly been trying to work on. I feel like becoming a hairdresser actually helped me break out of that a lot because, if y'all think I'm shy now, you should've seen me before when I was a server. I've always worked very social jobs, but I didn't really start to build my confidence personally until I started doing hair… until I was able to get behind the chair literally.

Figuratively, I was on the spot, but not on the spot because it was about them and not me. And I think that's one of the things I love about this job is we can excel, but it's all about everybody else. Like it's a service that we're doing.

That's why I wanted to educate from the beginning, but I went to hair school. I would attend probably 10-15 advanced education courses while in hair school, and I would go back to school and I would teach them... the teachers would call me up to teach the class. Even being as shy as I was, that made it to where I wasn't, at least in that scenario, because I could just share whatever I had been given.

☀

THE BEAUTY: I'm very, very sensitive to my own feelings and other people's feelings as well. I can empathize with other people's pain and their feelings. I'm able to listen to them and putting myself in their shoes and help them achieve what they want or direct them into the area that they want. I've been doing hair for 12 years, and I've been educating for 10 of those years; and when I'm doing hair, I'm so confident when I'm behind the chair. When I'm in my salon, my employees want me to come and do the consultation for them cause I'll just own straight up exactly how it is. Either you're going to get it or you're not.

☀ ☀

Kevin's Summary

Hey, y'all did a great job! I just want to close out by saying this right here: In our industry, everything ain't glitz and glamour, we are real people and we have our real fights, our real struggles. But we also have our REAL VICTORIES. And, that's what make the BEAST in the BEAUTY worth it all.

To watch the LIVE taping of the Behind the Scenes Interview, go to **bit.ly/beastinthebeauty**
Password Required: beast2020 (case sensitive)

CUT

style 2

The Evolution of the Beast

by Vicki Kirk May

I have encountered so many beastly situations, moments, etc., in my life I stopped trying to keep up. Realizing that the beast is going to show up or better yet, it *has* to show up, has changed how I show up in those moments when the beast seemed to be winning. I wanted to tuck tail and hide. I wanted to cry uncle. I wanted to throw in the proverbial towel and literally say the heck with it all!

For me, beastly moments brought out the beast in me. Thinking back on past behavior makes me squirm on the inside. My actions made everything worse. I did not know it then, but how I reacted to obstacles and trials in my life made them worse. I was not aware that I had the capacity to deal with my problems. Therefore I did not handle them in a mentally, emotionally, spiritually, relationally, and financially healthy manner.

The beasts, and that's beasts with an "s", seem to have vowed to kill, steal, and destroy all that I worked to achieve and I gave them what was needed to accomplish just that. Seems crazy but it is true. I handed the devil the gun and said *shoot*.

☀

Mentally I played mind games with myself. Every beastly, untrue, disparaging, deadly, unproductive, unfruitful, divisive word I could remember I played back with intention. It did not matter if it was spoken by me or others I hit the replay button over and over and over again ,until it became a never-ending song that got louder every time I messed up.

Emotionally I was all over the place. My mess-up tore at my heart. For a long time I didn't realize it but I allowed my trials to turn me against me. I had un-forgiveness in my heart towards me. A major revelation in my life was acknowledging that the person I had to forgive was myself. The person that I was mad at was me. The person I did not love was staring me back in the mirror.

My heart was broken and no one or no one thing could fix the beast that I invited in but me. Yep I invited the beast to come in and dwell every time I waddled in my mess, every time I stopped when things got rough, every time I backed paddled because of doubt, every time I took action to please others instead of God.

I wanted what I wanted. The heart deceived me on many occasions but I had to trust it again. I wasn't ready. At this point, I'm down one marriage, a repossessed car, a foreclosure, and a plummeting credit score.

☀

Comfort is what I longed for more than anything. I wanted immediate feel good. I'm in my thirties and I began a relationship that, over the course of many years, only made things worse. Food had become my best friend, my companion, my go-to drug of choice. Now of course even now, there might be some exaggeration, but the fact is I fell deeper in love with food when my life was not going as planned. Soon I not only had to deal with piecing my life together after my divorce and financial ruin, I was gaining weight like crazy. Years later I asked my sister why she did not tell me I had gotten so big. Needless to say love is blind!

☀

As you deal with trials that come in your life, you may do as I have done in the past, make them worse by beating up on yourself. You may even fall hard to the ground and just sit there a moment. It happens!

Most times the beast catches us off guard. Your business is booming. Clientele is at an all-time high. You have more money than you ever had, and BAM! You're sucker punched! Illness, divorce, death, accident, recession, etc., happens unexpectedly. What do you do? How do you handle the disruption in your life and business?

Spiritually, I began to doubt my relationship with God. I thought I wasn't worthy of more. The enemy was inside my head feeding my insecurities. Remember I previously said that I replayed those negative words until it became a song that got louder each time I messed up. On cue, the song played in my head. Thinking about it now ,I can hardly believe that I actually thought I did not deserve to have great things happen to me and for me.

What's your song? Is it "I'll never amount to anything." or is it "Good things don't happen to people like me"? Whatever the song is, just know that it's no longer a hit record. You deserve to be great and do great things and have great things happen in your life.

☀

THE PERCEPTION: Perception is key! If I wanted my life to change, I had to change. In some instances that meant make better decisions, in other cases that meant total elimination. In most cases that meant changing how I viewed things that were happening or had happened in my life.

I had to completely change my beliefs, values, and my attitude. It was not without trepidation.Evolution was scarier than the beast that initiated the change. No kidding, the trials that I faced in life were insurmountable but what I had to do to change and conquer what once conquered me was even greater.

The Evolution of the beast began! After 10 years I finally got the revelation… if I change *everything* changes! No longer did I believe I could kill the beast, wish the beast away, live such a great life that the beast would not show up. I HAD NO CONTROL OVER THE BEAST!

It was coming and there was nothing I could do about it. For me, to make sense of everything going on in my life I had to bring purpose to it. Where do I go for purpose? I go to the Word of God.

The beast causes sporadic temporary blindness. Its presence blinds us to the truth and illuminates the facts. During my episodes of sight, I ran to the Word of God. It was in the word that I began to understand the purpose of the beast. It is my desire to share with you how the very thing that seems insurmountable can evolve into a pebble powerful enough to create a ripple effect of change in you so that you can effectuate change in the world.

THE PURPOSE: First things first, get back to the basics. Stop over-complicating everything. Go back to what worked for you in the past. Going back to the basics means remember the "why" behind it all or at least understanding that there is a reason for what you are experiencing.

Getting back to the basics reminds you of what you are made out of. Think about it! You have not lost all your battles. Take time and think about your victories. What actions did you take so that you could experience success? Do that again!

For me, it was and still is my faith and belief in a power and source bigger than anything and everything that could possibly come to kill, steal, or destroy me. I call Him GOD.

I knew that there were answers that I was not allowing myself to attract. The disconnection was real and I had to reconnect. Studying the scriptures worked before so I did it again. It never fails. God's Word gives us the answer if we are willing to receive.

With much meditation, I found my scripture I would make a daily part of my life. Romans 8:28 (the New Living Translation) reads:

> *And we know that God causes everything to work together for the good of those who love God and are called according to His purpose.*

I needed a reason for the beast to show up. What God revealed to me in that one scripture changed how I perceived my beast. The beast was no longer the monster that came to hurt me. It was the conduit that God used to evoke a sincere praise from me while in the midst of my problems. Ultimately God would be glorified.

As I meditated on that scripture, it became evident that God was going to see to it that I win. Putting into practice what made me succeed in the past gave me the confidence to move forward. My renewed purpose had begun to change my perception of the beast. The evolution had started.

※

The awareness of purpose makes the beast less intimidating. With that awareness, however, I had to make sure that a less intimidating beast didn't become one that I now tolerated. Purpose was just the beginning of the evolution.

How you perceive the beast determines the power of the beast. Before the revelation that the beast showing up in my life has purpose, it was a monstrous, inhumane thing that appeared to be winning all the time. But now I can see it differently. Purpose changed my literal and spiritual perception of life's trials.

I remember reading the story of Joseph (I suggest you read the story) in the Bible. In that story, it showed me firsthand how God is truly the author and finisher of my faith. He is in control of your life and if He says it, that settles it. So no matter what comes your way just know that it is working for your good.

No matter what came Joseph's way, it was a set up for success. He was envied by his siblings, thrown in a pit, lied on by pharaoh's wife, put in jail all so he could succeed at fulfilling his destiny.

When you view your obstacles as pathways to your success instead of a punishment for past mistakes and disobedience, it frees you to fight for what you are believing God for. What you thought was a punishment in actuality was positioning. God's ways are not our ways. His thoughts are not are thoughts. He knows us better than we know ourselves. Because of His infinite wisdom, He allows turbulence to shake us up just enough to get our attention. Blinded by the beast of facts, most lose focus of the truth. The truth is the beast comes to show us the beauty.

※

THE POSITIONING: I wish I could say that you would no longer have to experience the beast. If you keep living, the beast shows up. If you keep dreaming, the beast shows up. If you keep hoping, the beast shows up. The beast is relentless, doesn't take a break, and will ride you until you say uncle.

However, I can reassure you that with the right moves, the trials you face will position you for great things to happen in your life. I know that this is very cliché-ish, but with every level comes a new devil. The beast comes to strengthen your hinds feet for the climb—not to trip you up. The trip comes when you are not prepared. The best way to defeat the beast is to expect it, welcome it, and embrace it when it comes. Your positive response weakens the power of the beast. Once weakened, you then can move into your promised position.

☼

Your position affects your perception. What you see on level one does not look the same from a higher altitude. While Joseph was in the pit he only saw at ground level. He was only able to make a difference from ground level. However when in the palace, he was able to make a major impact because of the power and authority that came with the position. If Joseph had not experienced his low moments, he would not have been prepared for the high.

While in my low moments, I could not pay any attention to anything but the fact that I was drowning and no help was in sight. God had to change my mind before I could understand that what did not kill me only made me stronger. Everything I thought was limiting me was God's way of protecting me from receiving the beauty of His promises prematurely.

☼

THE PROTECTION AND RESTRICTION: The beast is evolving! I know it! I could feel it, taste it, smell it! I was being engulfed by the transforming energy showing up as evolution. YES! I was evolving, but so was the beast. The stronger I became, the more authentic, the more courageous, the more powerful, and purposeful I showed up, but so did it [the beast].

As I evolved, what was then a beast was now a blessing. The interferences, blockades, and stumbling blocks were actually a shield of protection. During those times that I was out of alignment with God, trouble came and ushered me to the throne. When I implemented a good idea instead of a God idea without permission from God, hardships halted my movement.

God had issued a restraining order on my behalf and I did not even know it. It was those restrictions that protected my destiny. God double-dogged dared the enemy to harm me. Satan could only come so far and do so much before God intervened. My destiny was a stake. No way would God allow my destiny to be tampered with. But not only did He restrict who and what was out to me from reaching my destination, He also put some restrictions on me.

☀

It is imperative that you know God's restrictions on your life. It must be clear! Delays, postpones, cancellations continued to show up in my life because I did not honor

God's restraints. Now to my defense, as if I need it, I did not know my restrictions.

Adam and Eve were restricted from eating from the tree of life. Sampson could not put a razor to his head. For me, it is to honor the calling on my life to the fullest. I am to win souls to Christ. Whenever that takes a back seat to what I want to do, destiny is interrupted.

God has put a mandate on your life. What is that mandate? In order to get unstuck and move towards your destiny, you must adhere to the mandate God has placed on your life. It is only then the beast is harmless as a newborn baby.

❁

I thought it was the beast that had evolved. It did not look the same or feel the same. My revelation is the beast never changes. It fights even when defeated. It is relentless, never giving up, even when knowing its fate is failure.

My journey brought me to the realization that if I evolve, everything evolves. My spiritual father once told me the heart has changed, the mind is changing, and the body is waiting on change.

Everyday my prayer was "God renew my mind." There had to be a mental move towards destiny. I knew in my heart of hearts that I wanted to do better and be better. Nevertheless what my heart wanted did not always show up in my behaviors.

A renewed mind gave me a renewed purpose. The beast no longer has jurisdiction over my life. The restraining order was and still is in effect.

Truly, there is no doubt that The EVOLUTION OF VICKI caused the evolution of the beast!

ev·o·lu·tion

/ˌevəˈlo͞oSH(ə)n/

The process of formation, growth and development of oneself... to evolve

style 3

The Skin I'm In

by Jennifer Bowens

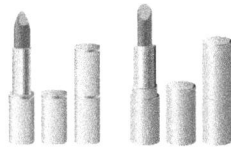

I grew up in a small town, smack dab in the middle of Georgia. My community is a rural area, where my race makes up only ten percent of the population. I'm thankful for my upbringing showing me to be open-minded and not stuck around people who only look like me.

It also helped to grow up in a Christian household. My family raised me to love everyone, as God does. There were no racial slurs in my household. My parents invited friends and coworkers from all different backgrounds to come by the house. This helped me and handicapped me. The handicap did not prepare me for the harsh reality of the rest of the world outside of my home.

In Cosmetology school, we had a diverse group of students and staff. We also serviced any client who came in to the school's salon. We could not pick and choose who we could service or what service we wanted. Students learned to style all hair types. I knew before I started school that I wanted to do all hair types.

Well, I got my reality check at my first salon job, and they only served one demographic. I only lasted one month. The first time I did someone's hair who wasn't White, the owner said something to me. She told me she didn't want all of those greasy products on her stuff. That let me know she really didn't understand textured hair!

I wasn't as confrontational as I am now. After my shift, I left but came back after the salon closed. I wrote a letter. I placed my key inside the envelope along with it.

I dropped out of Cosmetology school to work for her as an apprentice. I was almost finished with school! But I wanted to go ahead and start making money while I was in school. I took the fast path. Now I believe the door closed quickly to teach me a lesson.

I was so discouraged, I stopped doing hair for over five years. This was almost fifteen years ago.

In 2011, I felt in my spirit to start my Cosmetology journey again. When I feel something so heavily, I know it's Divine. I'm blessed with discernment, so I listen before I make a move.

Now, knowing and doing are two separate things. I used to be stubborn and strong-minded, but I'm much better now that I'm older.

I started providing friends and family hair services to build my portfolio and started school at the beginning of the following year. I kept my regular bartending job, and did the hair services around my work schedule.

My regular job paid the bills, with enough left over for savings. With five years of experience, I could pretty much walk into any restaurant or bar and walk out with a job.

Unfortunately, the bartending jobs came with a territory, cycles of partying then not partying. I would go out often partying for a few months, grow tired of the lifestyle, and take a few months off. I made sure to go to church on Sunday morning, though.

꽃

Two months before registration for school, I lost my bartending job. The restaurant received a citation earlier in the year. A previous bartender served alcohol to someone underage. The State sent someone undercover to see if it would happen again.

The person ordered a beer. I poured but I kept the glass behind the bar and asked for his I.D. He said he needed to go out to find it. An official came in to say I served him underage. I didn't serve him the beverage, but I still poured the beer upon his request. The restaurant received their second citation in six months and it caused them to receive a $10,000 fine. They had no choice but to fire me.

Once I was over the shock of actually leaving a job by force and not by choice, I walked out feeling peaceful. As this door closed, another one opened. I had to escape the never-ending partying cycle.

☀

A few days later, on my way to church, I passed by a sign which said "Hiring Stylists and Barbers". It caught my attention because I had been taking this same route every week, twice a week on the way to church. Somehow, I never realized there was a salon right there. It bothered me because, in our small town, we notice everything.

We had a guest speaker at church and the topic was "Knowing Your Purpose". It seemed like this speaker prepared the message for me! I kept getting distracted by thinking about the salon I passed by on the way. I told myself, "Girl, think about it when you leave, you might miss something important!"

I looked up and the speaker said, "If there is something so heavy on your mind right now that you can't even stay focused, it may be God trying to tell you your purpose!"

Y'all! It was a slap of reality! Everything he said was sent by God!

I have this journal that I take notes in for church. At the bottom of every page is an inspirational quote. I usually read it while I'm waiting for service to start, but I didn't that day, I waited until afterward to read it. The question asked, "Do you know your purpose in life?" Another slap in the face!

I left the church so on fire. I would call the salon number the next day. I took a picture of the "Hiring" sign on the way back home.

☀

The next day I called the salon. I let the phone ring twice and hung up when doubt started setting in. "She won't hire me without a license", "I never finished school", "I have no clientele", "These few pictures I'd taken over the last few months are not salon pictures. You can tell they are in someone's house".

The salon owner called me back. I was transparent about my situation. The more we talked, the more she put me at ease. I ended up sharing with her how I believed God sent me to call her.

She then shared that when she attended church yesterday, God told her not to worry about her situation. Turns out, we were at the same church hearing the same words!

Her fiance was in the military, which most of the time, meant not settling down in one area. They were moving out of state in the next couple of months. She wanted to staff the salon, so she didn't have to close it.

Being unlicensed, I didn't know how I fit into that vision, but God already worked it out.

A couple of days later, I called my close friend whom I met in Cosmetology school in 2004. We kept in touch over the years, on and off, but always picked up where we left off no matter how much time had passed.

She thought I called for her to style my hair. I told her about the conversation with the owner and how she needed stylists in the salon. I needed someone I could work under. She said she would pray and ask God about it. A few days later she received her answer.

☀

One month later, we received the keys to the salon and I sent in my paperwork to apprentice under her. We were working for the owner and started running the business for her. Everything made sense of why I was fired, why I felt deeply in my spirit to take portfolio pictures, and why I met my friend seven years prior.

I thought I would be finishing school, but our plans are not always what we think they are. An apprenticeship would take longer than me finishing school, but I knew I was exactly where I needed to be.

Two months later, the owner offered me the opportunity to buy out the salon. It was too much for her to pay bills outside of the state and keep up with everything. The price she offered me was everything I had in savings minus two dollars and some change.

That was confirmation the salon was for me! I accepted the price.

When I discussed my decision with my family, I started doubting myself. "How are you going to own a salon and you're not licensed yet? You need to do things in order. You're not ready. You just started building your clientele. How are you going to own a salon without any clients?"

Fear set in. Those questions kept me from seeing the signs in front of me! I can't blame my family for questioning me either. I was a three-time college drop out and on my second apprenticeship. I didn't always make the best decisions growing up. I took risks and did not care about society's standards. I've learned characteristics don't have to be flawed. You just have to learn how to use them positively.

A few weeks went by, and I procrastinated on making a decision. My significant other at the time had to give me a reality check. He had to remind me of everything that was set before me. This was the right thing to do. I would be crazy to NOT do it. Those questions from family were still in the back of my mind, though. I was stubborn.

☀

The next week, someone came in to view the salon for purchase. I learned an expensive lesson about procrastination and doubt. We ended up being in a bidding war and the salon cost me $1,000 more than the original offer. But it was finally mine!

When we don't move when God says move, I guarantee life will force you to make a move or get out of the way for someone else.

I spent all of my money. My lovely friend now became my business partner. I wouldn't have trusted anyone else to be the one.

Our business name came to me and as soon as I said it to her, she agreed. This whole journey was divinely designed from the beginning. We named the business "Divine Designs Salon".

After a few months of getting all the bills transferred in our names, business paperwork with licensing together, and having inspections, we celebrated our grand opening on July 14, 2012.

It is still surreal when I think about it. Just months after being fired from my job, I owned my own business!

⚙

Running a diverse business came with challenges. Remember, I grew up being a minority in my community. My business partner grew up in the military and was used to being around lots of different people. She even lived outside of the United States. Keep in mind, I'm White and she is Black.

People would come in and see us doing the hair of those who didn't look like us, or have hair like us. People told us that we were opposites. Some said we needed to trade clients. So many people said this!

But being located in a small town, there are lots of people who haven't lived outside of that town or not far from there. Sometimes that can leave people to not be as open to diversity because they've never experienced other cultures.

We didn't care. We encouraged and celebrated diversity. Our logo represented a beautiful woman. On one side of her head, she had straighter hair that grew downward. On the other side, she had curly hair that grew outward. The person that designed it captured our brand.

⚙

Two years later, my business partner had another career calling. Her career has been her ministry. And I can't argue with God.

I completed my apprenticeship and passed my state boards. I received my Master Cosmetology license. We had also built a team of people, so I had booth renters to help with salon bills.

She didn't leave me hanging at all. I thanked her and God for the time we had together.

When people would walk in that looked like her, they would walk straight to her. She would explain how I better suited their hairstyle preference. And a lot of the times, vice versa.

Our clients trusted our recommendations. I didn't realize how much we depended on each other until she left. That's when I experienced adversity.

My clientele grew as social media became more and more popular. People would book me from seeing my clients' pictures posted on social media. When they would enter the salon and see me, a lot of the times they looked so confused. The biggest question would be, "You are so-and-so from Facebook/Instagram?"

Some people would stay, some people would change their minds and leave.

One time, a lady insisted on explaining why a White person would NEVER touch her hair! To diffuse the situation, I kept saying, "please, have a good day," but she would not leave until she made her point.

She was adamant that everyone in the salon heard what she had to say because she stood at the door while stating matter of factly her case. I was so embarrassed, I really just wanted her to leave instead of carrying on in front of all of my team members.

Looking back, I missed the opportunity to have a progressive conversation. I was trying to avoid confrontation, to stay professional.

But with the help of my team members, who were also people of color, we could have used that platform to help open her mind.

Not to get me to do her hair, but to allow her to voice her feelings without being silenced. And hopefully, she would have given me the same chance.

Back then, I wasn't as experienced with controlling a salon environment or speaking up. For centuries, people of color have been silenced, and I showed her I was just like any other White person she has probably encountered.

☼

Using your platform as a way to promote diversity and unity is work. It's not comfortable at times and it can get ugly. But it is TOTALLY necessary if you are servicing clients who do not look like you.

And most of the time it has beautiful outcomes. You must first educate yourself and get to know other people from other backgrounds.

I haven't always gotten it right. Every day is a learning experience when it comes to cultural appropriation. You may say something that doesn't sit right, but that leaves room for correction and growth. It is better than not speaking up at all.

☀

If you ever get to a point where you've reached a brick wall, put on the brakes. Some people look at 'different' as either right or wrong, instead of just what it is… different.

Unfortunately, there are people that are closed-minded. End that chapter and make room. Some people will put up barriers because of racial differences no matter what you do or say.

But, as long as there is a level of respect, it can be a great opportunity to open our minds!

☀

Now that we've handled the social side of business, let's get on the FISCAL side!

☞I learned that referrals are the best form of advertisement for me. It gives that level of trust I always want for my customers. I also make sure to take pictures of my work to keep my portfolio up-to-date. It lets potential clients see styles before they book. If the picture doesn't look as good as it does in-person, don't post it.

By the time I reached my third year of business, I had to turn people down from being so booked. Just from referrals and social media.

I now control the type of clients I want. And those clients are open-minded, respectful, and care about the health of their hair as much as I do!

☀

I'll admit, desperation for clients made me put up with certain things. I thought I needed the money no matter how people treated me.

☞I learned and grew from that person. You cannot put a price on peace and you do not need anyone's money who doesn't respect you.

☞Don't let your clients fall into the habit of being late. But you better be timely too! Don't let them be no-shows without consequences. Don't let sly remarks go unchecked. And don't let them change the atmosphere of your environment!

☞When you have diversity in your salon, there will be adversity at times. You must be prepared for potential conflict.

☞And as far as my salon owners go, if team members that won't align with your vision, find a new team. If you aren't in an environment that aligns with your vision, find a new environment. I heard people say, "Not all money is good money." Don't downgrade your position. Know your value and worth.

You run your business. Do not let that business run you. Take charge.

And if you really want a diverse salon, make sure you're mentally capable of diving into that pool.

beau ·ti ·ful
/byoo-tuh-fuhl/

Possessing qualities that give great pleasure
or satisfaction to see, hear, think about, etc.;
delighting the senses or mind

style 4

The Good, The Bad, The Ugly

by Ashley Hawkins

The Good

Let's start from the beginning! January 31, 1993 was the day the world stood still. It felt as if an earthquake shook the whole world at the same time. Some thought the end was near, so they repented for comfort; others thought a war had launched.

No, it wasn't an earthquake, nor war, but it was the world spinning forward in the right direction for the first time because everything on earth had been backwards. Had the

Messiah returned? No, this was the day that Ashley Michelle Hawkins was born.

Ever felt like you were born for a bigger purpose other than you being the only sperm that made it to the egg? I felt that way since day one.

※

A little about my back story… I was born and raised in a small town called Florence, South Carolina. Yes, the South! Don't remind me. I have two loving parents—who really tried their best—and two sisters, but I only grew up with one. Have you ever felt like the black sheep in your family?

I learned to embrace it. At the age of four, my father decided to change his life for the better and wanted to "give back" to his community. You see, before he was an addict and did jail time.

Now, my father was literally the Martin Luther King, Jr. of Florence. He had summer camps, Juneteenth events, Black History Parade, and he was a basketball coach and mentor to younger male and females in the community.

My mom would always make sure we donate our used items and time to help our local citizens. So, I guess you can say *giving* is in my blood.

Growing up, there was a lot of pressure to be perfect because of who my father was. I often felt as if I had to walk on eggshells, which taught me to keep things to myself.

As a child I had lots of friends, but I knew I could not share everything—even with them. I have a sister who is 9 years older than me, whom I was told asked for a little sister. There was a pretty significant age gap, so it made sense why most said I acted older for my age.

I hope you can understand that my parents had me later in life, meaning they were real old school. Well, here I am, 26 years old, single, childless and building a successful business.

I grew up "Hood Rich" as most people call it, meaning we were not rich by any means, but to say we lived in the hood, we were financially comfortable. What makes it hood is by my father making his money on his own. My father would be who you called a hustler—he can make a dollar out of 15 cents.

From that lifestyle, I grew to love money and began to understand how it worked. Because everyone around me was a felon, they had to create their own jobs. They took a negative situation and made it positive. I guess, to a certain extent, I agree with the concept; but then I often asked myself, "What got a man there in the first place?"

I learned over the years to understand that I could have easily made the same choice. I learned to be a problem solver, do not complain or get stuck, figure how to get out.

☀

As a child, I knew I wanted to be great! To me, that meant to have my name in lights and be able to make a major difference in the world. Make my human existence mean something.

Furthermore, I knew I wanted to be successful and wealthy, afford whatever and be able to help whomever whenever I wanted to. The only problem was… how do I *get* there?

Starting a business where I'm from was nothing or, shall I say, starting a *side hustle*. As a kid, I did nails, sold cooked food, and even "burned" CDs. I did it all.

I understood how to make a dollar, or at least I thought. But having a legitimate business was always my goal. I always loved the idea of becoming an entrepreneur with no one telling me what to do.

I wanted to provide jobs within my community to provide a sense of stability for those in need. Most importantly, I desired to help build generational wealth.

The Bad

When I was younger, I loved going to the hair salon. Do not get me wrong, I didn't like having to stay there all day, but I enjoyed watching the hair stylists work.

It was like being in a candy store. I loved how you can see a picture and put on a canvas [the client]. I would dream that I could do the same one day. I would ask people to teach me how, some would but majority would not. It was at that point that I realized hair was something that I wanted to do, and wouldn't mind learning on my own. I did not have the hopes to be hair stylist, more so learn to do certain styles, and I knew that meant going to cosmetology school.

I was beginning and had absolutely no idea of the countless hours and State board license exams that waited ahead. I figured hair school would just teach me the latest styles. Oh, how I was mistaken!

Initially, I wanted to be a famous fashion designer; fashion was my passion. I loved placing pieces together. Overall, I craved to be in the beauty industry, this was my calling. The entire canvas, head to feet. I wanted my own fashion line so badly! Even have my own skincare line, hair salon, and beauty supply store.

☀

My dreams are pretty much still alive, but everything has its process. Even though this may sound positive, it is sometimes hard to stay in the position. There are times you feel as if nothing will ever work out.

After my freshman year of high school, my life changed. When I was 15 years old, my mom left us. But it had always been me and my father, so it did not feel any different really. The part that hurt the most was the fact that I always yearned for my mother's affection, but at that moment, I knew it would never happen.

I expressed that hurt through anger, I would quickly jump from 0 to 100. The school guidance counselor suggested I take a "test" and it indicated I was depressed. At 15 years old.

Perhaps I have been in that space for a long time and had to learn to release. I thought I was comfortable during my freshman year of high school. I had two boyfriends—an athletic, football playing boyfriend and the "bad boy" type of boyfriend. I developed habits from them both, some that even left me emotionally unattached. Not to mention I'm still dealing with my parent's divorce. I tried not to get caught up in feelings.

And, because I wasn't supposed to date until 17, I didn't dare do anything *extra* with a boy that would result in having babies.

Yes, my mother was gone, but I still had my dad. All wasn't totally lost. But deep inside, I mourned that loss. As a kid, I expressed it through outbursts, getting into trouble, disrespecting adults, just wilding out. Through it all, now I realize as an adult, I was just trying to find myself. And every road pointed back to hair.

Although I didn't play sports like my father would have liked, I participated in more academic competitions. I was the vice president of the freshman academy, and a member of the Future Business Leaders of America (FBLA) and ROTC my ninth grade year.

I always took advantage of any programs that would help me get far. That same year, there was a cosmetology program held at my local community center. The Cosmetology Instructor at Florence Darlington Technical College, Mrs. McKnight, co-instructed us along with her daughter. They taught the fundamentals and knowledge of the beauty industry. Plus, she was trying to give back to her community by keep young ladies off the streets or from becoming pregnant.

My mom usually paid for me to get my hair done, after she left, I had to pay myself. A teenager with no job, YouTube became my best friend, and I decided to do my own hair— I will have to learn one day.

Can I tell you a secret? ... I thought hairstylist were born with this gift, I did not realize you had to put in work. And people will be so quick to tell you that it is *ugly*, little do they know!!

To this day, I feel that you should not disrespect anyone that does your hair or cook your food. Believe me, they have the upper hand!

Even though my hair was looking like who did it and why, I knew I had to learn. Even then, I felt like a stylist.

In conclusion, that's where it all started.

☀

Growing up my father was militant and was trying to groom us so we could handle the military. I recall he wanted me and my sister to go into the military, as he stated that he could not afford to send us to college. Even though I had the secret hope of becoming a stylist, my freshman year of high school landed me in The Reserve Officer Training Corps (ROTC). The plan was to complete all four years, then go to the Air Force. This was something I did not want to do, but I was open to it.

I guess the universe understood my heart's desire, so for my sophomore year I was not placed back in ROTC. Okay, I thought, maybe this could be my time to complete cosmetology. So, I finally asked my guidance counselor if I'd be able to register for cosmetology. She stated that I was to start my freshman year, and at that time, I would have to pick something else.

☀

Once again, I felt as though a curve ball was thrown. As you can imagine, I was all over the place with emotions and career path. So instead of cosmetology, I started culinary arts. And boy was that a completely different turn! But do not get me wrong, I enjoyed cooking because I felt culinary arts was a way to be fancy with cooking. Who does not love to be fancy?

My sophomore year, I was presented the opportunity to be a part of a summer business competition at Francis Marion University, a local college in my area. I was one out of 20 students in my high school to be a part of that journey. Of course, my industry of choice was fashion. This was the chance to showcase my skills. My main designs were distress and bleached jeans with curve support. I wanted to win!

Most of students dropped out and became argumentative with the instructor. On competition day, we must present our business plan to investors, I was confident I was going to win. I had a good relationship with the teacher, so naturally I thought she would have put in extra brownie points for me.

There were three places, and I didn't win either. I was so confused. I felt that I worked harder than my fellow classmates. Yes, call me a sore loser, but I couldn't handle the loss and called my father to come pick me up. I played to win; who doesn't want to win? That is why I hate competitions; in an ideal world, I feel everyone should win.

My father and teacher expressed my lack of sportsmanship as I didn't stay to support to my classmates. Not trying to sound petty, but they did not even talk to me.

The instructor told me that the final decision would be hers. I could not understand why I did not win anything. Fudge it, if I don't win, no one does. Harsh right?

Well, call me cocky but I feel as if no one wants to win as bad as me. What do I mean by that? I strive everyday to be successful, paved the way, take care of my family.

Others just want to get by, so it annoys me to be beside someone who isn't passionated the way I am. My component just want to win to look cool, I want to win to feed everyone and their mother.

I was raised by the idea of we (Black people) do not win individually, but as a whole. So imagine for a second, Harriet Tubman freeing herself and no one else... yeah, I can not.

But I had to realize my flaws and grow from that. Maybe one day a hair competition, but never take my eyes off the prize.

☼

Fast forward to senior year—the year I hated school! I reached the point where the stress of school overrode my love for learning. I always said I was leaving school at 17, diploma or not! That was the legal age to dropout. Nonetheless, I knew I had to get a diploma, but I still wanted to leave. School became more about finding emotional security and meeting someone else who felt the same way.

I met my friend, Amber, that year as well and she told me about the early graduation process. My thoughts ran and I began planning to get my diploma and get out of there. She advised me to speak with my guidance counselor about my credits so I can graduate in January of 2011.

So, we went to the guidance office together and saw this lady. She really did not want us to graduate early, but I indeed had enough credits to do so.

Talking to my father was interesting as he did not agree either. "Oh well," I thought. I had to finish school at some point, so I decided to graduate in January. Amber came up with the idea to apply to colleges and start in January (the fall semester) so way we could graduate high school in December.

At first, we did not take researching colleges seriously as we didn't care what school accepted us. We just couldn't wait to get out of high school. Then, one day, it hit that we were about to embark on our journey into adulthood, and time then was very crucial. I personally did not have the taste for college, I just wanted to be an entrepreneur, start my own clothing line and do hair here and there.

In this small town, success did not start unless you owned land or worked in a factory plant. And fashion designing industry was almost non-existent in that area. At that point, I wanted to get far away from South Carolina as possible and never look back. But the question was, how?

☀

One afternoon Amber and I visited the school library to search for colleges on the internet. I searched fashion design schools near me, and there it was, right in my face: The Art Institute of Charleston. I could not believe it! Charleston was only two hours away from where I lived. Okay this might work. I applied and was accepted to the institute.

I did it! One of only a group of four students! Graduation was December 17, 2010, and my start date for college was January 6, 2011. I had it all figured out... Move to

Charleston, stay on campus for one year, move to New York the next year to work for a designer company, and become a famous fashion designer and hairstylist. Sounded like a solid plan to me.

Bags packed, ready to go! New journey, new city, new beginnings. Or so I thought. Because my mom and dad couldn't afford the tuition, my new beginnings ended real fast. Even with the plan to work once I got to school still wouldn't work because the tuition was too expensive. So just like that, I thought my dream had been crushed. Nevertheless, I had hope. I had no choice but to.

I contemplated becoming a local designer; you know, start off small. I moved to Lexington, South Carolina to stay with my cousin to start college and a new job. Well, that was more of her [my cousin] plan, I was just looking at schools, but she had my life figured out.

My cousin had everyone's life figured out. Let's just say my stay lasted about a week before it was time to leave her and never look back. She was super religious and it was either her way or no way. I sadly moved back to Florence and started Florence Darlington Tech. Since technically I was still a "high school" student, I qualified for the Bridge Program—taking college classes on a high school level. What a month it was!

I wanted to do the bridge program in high school, but transportation became an issue. I then inquired about the one-month cosmetology program that was due to start in

October. But that was a no-go, so I chose Business Management. I was faced with yet another roadblock—no fashion, no hair. I lost complete interest in school and truth be told, I did not care.

My family felt I was wasting time, and even my life. If it were up to them, I would've joined the military and became a nurse. But that life was not for me. I wanted to touch people, not their bodily fluids. I can be so extra, and yet I gave in. I researched medical programs, and to my surprise, I liked the curriculum. I located Medjas Medical Training Center and applied.

Still enrolled at Tech, they did not offer this program at the time. Instead of explaining to the school that I will no longer attend, I did the mature adult thing; I left. I was surrounded by people who supported me and wanted to see me win. I was financially set. At the age of 18, I was a working woman selling Avon and marijuana.

☀

In South Carolina, there was nothing else to do...hell, you're farming anyway. It was the matter of what I wanted to do with my life and how to get there.

The training center did not provide financial aide. But paying was not a problem for me. I felt as though this was the start I needed; a good paying job to invest for cosmetology school in October.

I continued to hang with my friends, make money, smoke and chill all day with my boyfriend. I was a trooper; I had it all planned out in a matter of a month. Well until…

The Ugly

The owner of the class kept pushing the start date, she was trying to give other potential students the opportunity to sign up. The class was pushed from October to December of 2011. In the meantime, I just continued on with my usual day-to-day.

My father was the neighborhood bootlegger, since I was 18 at the time, I basically had to help run the family business. My father had been a bootlegger since I was 8, so it seemed really natural to me. But honestly, no one wants that lifestyle. You must deal with drunks all day, especially on Sundays because the liquor store is closed, deal with people stealing and or want a discount.

My father seemed to hate what he was doing, but, he had to do what he had to do. He was a great father. Even to this day, if I were to date a guy that seemed like my father, ironically my mother would say, "He acts just like your father, so that should workout."

❋

But I wanted the complete opposite. I was still dating my ex, who we will call Calvin. He was in the streets, but not recklessly, that's just what raised him. He was very protective and loyal, and to this day we are still friends.

Back to the school situation and pushing the date. The owner decided to finally push the start date to January 2012. By that time, I felt like I had a whole year off and did not do anything. Not even register for cosmetology classes. In my eyes everything has perfect timing, although we do not like to see it that way.

In April of 2011, my father brought me my first car, a 1989 Mercury Grand Marquis. Now that was my kind of ride. My family wondered why would I want a big body car like that? That was the era of old school coming back and I loved older cars. I often told people I loved my cars like I loved my men—old; but not too old just to be clear.

Anyway, from April to December, that old car caused a lot of stress. I was arrested in that car, my car was keyed, and someone even peed on it. Why? Honestly, I was a female trying to play a man's game.

❋

I was being "hated on" like the young folks like to say. And this ultimately costed me my life. Well, lets back track, growing up my house was always broken into, people figured we had money and I guess wanted to see if it was true.

It was hard to come and find your house in shambles and put the pieces back together. My father was now a patrol officer, so he felt that it was his duty to give everyone another chance because he was also that young man at one time. But little did he know, that type of kindness would cost him his life.

The story goes that a boy and his friends would break in when no one was home, and the neighbors saw nothing. Because of the "no snitch" rule, police were called for a report to send to insurance and we continued to live our lives as if nothing happened.

One day I saw the guy who broke in our home wearing my shoes, but my father would insist to let it go. I was ready to hurt someone. My father's excuse was that he promised me as a child that he would not go back to jail. Like mentioned earlier, my father was an addict and constantly going back and forth to jail, even when he got clean. I understood the promises a person could make to their child, all because of my father.

One night I was told repeatedly that someone was on my car. I finally decided to go outside. Some people in those environments are not even human anymore as they become products of their environments. So, I did not go outside alone.

I had a knife and pepper spray on me that my boyfriend, Calvin, gave me. I spoke with the person who was insisting that my car was his and belong to the hood. He was trying to show off for some girls, who were just as silly to think that would work. Long story short, I sprayed him, but not without feeling the effects! So of course, everyone scattered, and I ran in the house to get the spray out of my eyes because the wind blew some back in my face.

The following week my neighbor around the corner had their door kicked in. Unfortunately, he and his family were robbed at gun point. Stress, confusion, and worry became my new normal. My father said if they could do that to the neighbor, they could do it to us. My neighbor around the corner felt as if it was my next-door neighbor, and so did everyone else.

At that moment my boyfriend told my father war was coming and he needed to plan something to do. So, Calvin volunteered to be on house watch with his pistol, whenever we needed him. One night, my father had a DJ gig; yes, my father wore many hats, and I asked could my boyfriend stay and keep company.

My father, being cautious like most parents first said no, but eventually agreed. Calvin felt funny that whole night, it's like he could sense something bad was going to happen. Me being nonchalant wasn't helping. I cut off all of the lights and the television.

Calvin ordered me to go to my room with the crowbar and keep quiet. Suddenly there was a knock on the door, now being under the circumstances, we were not in business that night, so we had no clue who stood on the other side.

Calvin looked out the window and saw five guys dressed in all black, head to toe. Calvin stood there looking through the peak hole but their faces were covered. I could see it in his eyes that he was ready to go to war for me. He pulled out his pistol and stood watch until they eventually left.

When my father returned, we told him what happened, which he seemed very blasé about. I could not understand, like that was supposed to be us. Maybe he knew that he could not win. Being that my father was a felon, he could not buy a legal gun, so his friend gave him other options.

‎ ‎ ‎ ‎ ‎ ‎ ‎ ‎ ‎ ‎ ‎ ☼

Calvin and I are still friends. That night, he was willing to die for me. He also suggested to get guns because if something happened, I needed to be prepared. Little did he know, back in the day, men had respect for each other that was why they fought straight up, no weapons. But these days, in my opinion, guys hunger for blood.

The plan was to chill around the end of the year, then on the 2nd of January, I was to get a shotgun. On New Year's Day, after my family left, we began to prepare for the next day. My father sent me this chain text that said "I love you". I was upset with my father, for whatever reason I cannot remember. I opened my room door and told him, "I love you," not knowing that would be the last time.

☀

In the bathroom, there was a knock at the front door, I didn't hear my father go to the door, so I did not worry about it. Then there was another knock, as I was walking to the door I remember thinking how my dad had a peek hole on the front door, but I was too short to see through it without some type of assistance.

I began to open the door, and to this day, I regret that I did… A guy I know from my school rushed in the door and went straight to the kitchen. A masked man in all black entered the living room, pointed a gun at me and demanded to know 'where the money was'.

Now, at this time, all I could remember is Calvin placing a crowbar by the front door to my room and how he was taking me to buy my first shotgun the next day. How could I be so foolish? The hood don't take days off! The streets never sleeps.

As I am trained to say, 'I don't know where the money is', the masked intruder came closer to me with the gun and yelled, 'Get on the ground!"

I backed up, trying to think quick. I thought to yell out to my dad, but then I thought if he came running with no form of protection and this guy's gun is already out, my father would have been shot on impact, then this guy would have shot me. That plan won't work. Think quick!

So I continued to back up and then laid on my stomach. With the quickness, I heard footsteps of someone running. I don't know who it was.

Then I heard gun shots, and those same footsteps running again. At that moment I told myself, well this is it. I knew I was going to die and, to be honest, I felt like it was all I ever waited for.

My whole eighteen years of existence, I always asked 'why am I here?', like why me? Why this family? Why this life? Body? Attitude? And so forth... I suffered from depression long before that school therapist told me.

Deep inside, I was suicidal, and felt that was the time to go. I heard the intruder say, "What do we do with her?"

I didn't hear the other guy. Then I heard him say, "We cant just leave one."

At that moment, I searched my thoughts for reason to fight for my life, and I couldn't find one. I thought to myself, as long as my niece and boyfriend know I love them... that's all.

Suddenly, I heard footsteps walking out the door, I immediately jumped to my feet and ran as fast as I could to find my father. As I ran down the hallway, I saw his lifeless body on the floor leading to his bedroom.

I saw the bullet holes in his head, but I knew my dad was a fighter, so I knew he would get through this. I also heard him breathe, so I was trying to keep hope alive.

Tearing flying down my face, I quickly ran to the living room to grab the house phone. I then pulled out my cellular phone and called my boyfriend while dialing 911 on the house phone—so I could explain to them both what happened at the same time.

Everything seemed so surreal and I wanted to wake up from a nightmare. But this was real. It was happening. I walked out on the porch with the phones in my hands. A customer was coming towards the house, but from the look on his face, he didn't know what was going on. I looked to my right at our neighbors, who were standing on the porch and immediately I knew they had something to do with it. The coming days would prove me right.

That whole night was chaotic as you can imagine. My father was rushed to the hospital, but I had to stay at the house and answer questions from the detective. Other family members and friends went to the hospital, where my father passed shortly after arriving.

Actually, the detective told me that when I heard my dad breathe while he was laying on the floor, he was taking his last breath.

Now it is year 2020 and I am so blessed to have this opportunity, along with other beauty professional, to write my story. To be honest, most of my support has come for individuals I don't know. Crazy how things happen, but it happens for a reason.

I am 27 years old now, I started my clothing jean line on my birthday in May 2020. Let me give you a brief description of my year: January, I started and stopped working at H&R Block. I learned that when change is coming, it doesn't let you know, it just appears. My passion for taxes and that company quickly changed.

I am still not currently in a salon because I took 2019 to focus on other adventures instead of hair, and also with this corona virus going on. Depending on when you read this book, I lived through one of the most historic times of the global pandemic of COVID19, also known as the corona virus. So no, no one is in the salon right now! We are all under quarantine all across the world.

So I have time now to really focus on my next move. I am strategizing on how to expand AshleyMichellellc—my goal is to open my own beauty supply store within the next 12 months. With this free quarantine time I have decided to start other adventures like candle making, investing in stocks and real estate, focusing on becoming a better woman and person in general.

☀

On my journey, there seemed to be so much turmoil, confusion, stumbling, and trials. But, I had to learn to bear witness to the growth process and the matriculation that comes with evolution.

The good, the bad, and the ugly are areas in life that aren't meant to last, they're meant to test and develop. If it weren't for my experiences with everyone in my life, I wouldn't have made it through knowing how to cope with life's transformations as I transformed into the woman I am today, Ashley Hawkins.

"I strive everyday to be better than the last." -Ashley

em ·pow ·er

/əmˈpou(ə)r/

To give someone or self the authority or permission to do something

style 5

Make-up and Love Yourself: God Has A Plan For Your Pain

by Erika Nicole Lawson King

When I got married in 2008, I felt like that was at the beginning of my life. I felt like my life couldn't get any better. I had a big, beautiful wedding and I knew I was gonna live in a fairytale dream. But what do you do when it all falls apart? When that fairytale marriage comes to an end?

✺

Let me go back to the beginning… When I met my husband, I felt that I had found the missing puzzle in my life, he was perfect to me.

We loved all of the same things, we were both singers, both in the church, both worship leaders, we could finish each other's sentences, our birthdays were even the same day. He was my best friend… Perfect!

I was so in love with him until he became my everything, I lived to please him and make him happy. Neither one of us had children so I was excited about being able to give him his first child.

I remember when we were preparing for the wedding, I would do a lot of self-care things—I lost 30 lbs., exercised, drank water, spent time with my mom to learn how to become a wife—again, I wanted to please him.

I had found the happiness I had dreamed about my entire life. Then one day I looked up and I had a big beautiful ring on my finger, I had a marriage license, but I did not have a marriage.

I did not have the love and care of the man that I loved and was married to. I was devastated. I found myself trying to see what I did that was so bad that he did not love me anymore.

What mistakes had I made as a wife? What could I have done differently as a wife?

I found myself writing him letters and begging for his love, to all he never responded.

I allowed myself to be dumbed down and ran over in an effort to hold on to him. My life became about loving him and not loving myself. My self-esteem was in the toilet, I began to eat my hurt away and I found all of the weight I had lost and then some, which caused my self-esteem to drop even lower.

Women began to confront me about my own husband, women that wanted my position as his wife, women that knew me because we were all in the same church. I did not handle that level of disrespect with grace, believe me, I didn't... I was always in fight mode.

I had built up a wall of anger, I was always defensive and ready to fight at the drop of a dime. I had a friend, Bridget Earl Prichett, prophesied to me during that time and she told me that she knew my heart towards my marriage and that I desired to have my marriage, but God was going to snatch me out of the marriage. She said I was going to cry and be hurt, but when I dried my tears, I needed to raise my hands and tell God 'thank You'.

I heard her, but I didn't want to hear her. I wanted my husband, I wanted my marriage, I was going to fight harder, I wasn't going to leave my marriage without a fight.

I found myself separated in 2010 and divorced in 2012. I always say I found myself because, honestly, I was trying to find out how I got to these places and spaces in life. Nothing made sense to me. My emotions were everywhere. I was hurt, broken, lost, destroyed... just a total wreck.

I thought that we were going to live happily ever after. I did not know that forever would come to an end. How does forever come to an end?

The big beautiful wedding has now become a total waste of time for me. I was angry, bitter, hurt and embarrassed. The hurt intensified every time I went somewhere and they would introduce me as his wife, and I would have to correct them and say that we were divorced. Another stab in the wound if you know what I mean.

I would be brave in the moment, but inside I was crying my very heart out, I felt ashamed and disgraced.

I never got the opportunity to experience marital bliss, it was taken from me. And that opportunity to give my husband his first child was taken from me as well—he moved on with his life without me, and someone else gave him what I desired to be the only one to give him... a child.

He went on to have a family without me, the family that we were supposed to have. He gave my dream... my life to someone else.

Seeing him with his first child almost killed me, literally. I would cry for hours at a time until I was dehydrated with no more water left in my body. It literally almost killed me.

I continued to serve on the praise team at church, in which he was the leader; I submitted myself to an authority that mentally and emotionally abused me and honored him as my leadership.

Sunday after Sunday I would stand on that pulpit and lead God's people into worship; people would come up to me after service and tell me that I blessed them; then I would get in my car by myself and cry all the way home.

I was trying to be brave before the people and worship God with all that I had; all the while, I was bleeding inside and wondering why God had allowed this to be in my life.

Sometimes when you work in ministry, not being okay is not okay for you because the people need you. I was alone, hurt, bitter, and lost with no direction. I always walked around with my head held down in defeat. I even began to believe that death was better than my reality, this could not be real life or the abundant life that God said he had for me.

※

I recall working in a hair salon with my dear friend Ki Edwards; she did all she could to encourage me. I even remember one day she told me that she didn't look forward to coming to work with me because she knew I was gonna be sad. But honestly, I didn't know any other way to be. I didn't know how to be okay. I didn't know how to be happy. I didn't know how to be healed from the situation that was happening to me. It was hurtful, painful and unfair. I tell people that divorce is a different kind of hurt. Not that it hurts more, it hurts differently.

※

When I went through a divorce I had to give up my hopes and dreams for that union. This was a covenant with God that was being broken, one flesh now being torn in two, being left with resentment and feeling like I had failed. I then felt like the people around me didn't understand what I was truly bearing.

TRANSPARENT TRUTH MOMENT: When going through tough times, you find out who your real friends are. I found out the hard way that some of our mutual friends were just his friends and I could not trust them—real friends won't allow you to be blindsided by situations that can destroy you.

I had friends that I trusted and considered family, who would talk to me daily as a means of being there for me, then take what they learned and gossip about me thus putting my business in the street, or should I say, putting my business around the church.

Those friends that were my listening ear were also that talking mouth. I even had friends who later on were bold enough to tell me that during my hard times, they were never my friend… they just tolerated me. That hurt me to my core.

I honestly did not know who to trust, I felt so alone.

But God sent me what I like to call "trauma nurses" in the form of Spiritual Mothers. One had already walked my path, so she held my hand and walked me through this upsetting process.

The experience provoked me to do two things: (1) get closer to God and (2) dive deeper into my work. I submitted myself to my Pastors, Dr.'s Willie B. and Patricia O'Neal at Mt. Canaan Full Gospel Church, as they spiritually guided me towards my healing; along with my Mother Elder Anita Woody Lawson, My Auntie who is now my Angel in Heaven, Phyllis Woody Melton, and four awesome Spiritual Mothers that prayed for me day and night, BeBe Jefferson, Prophetess Glennitta Battle, Elder Faye Speed and Linda Stallworth.

The hurt that permeated my inner core didn't seem to oppress me as much anymore. This group of supportive individuals guarded my spirit and rebuilt me through prayer. They allowed me to call them, cry to them, vent to them and they always encouraged me to hold my head up high and not be ashamed about my situation.

They prayed for me without ceasing and guided me. My life seemed to change. I began to have peace. The happiness returned back into my life, and I started to do things that fulfilled me; things that made me have purpose again.

※

One thing that was rekindled was my love for doing makeup. I began to apply a little makeup to myself here and there. I started to gain the attention of a lot of people that knew I could do it a little because I always kept my makeup done. I tried to keep busy to say the least, so I thought might as well do something that I like to do.

I remember that year, I offered makeup services to many of my clients who were going to the prom that year. The more I did makeup, the more I fell in love with it; the more it became my favorite thing to do. I found myself slowly drifting away from doing hair and gravitating towards makeup.

But one thing I have learned in this industry is that some people will know that you have the potential of being good at something, rather than wanting to see you come up, they will do everything in their power in order to keep you down. But it has also taught me that man's rejection of you is God's opportunity to redirect your life.

※

During this time makeup and makeup artists (MUAs) were starting to become more and more popular. I began to gravitate toward friends who were doing makeup to see what I could learn. I attended their classes which stimulated me to even host a class or two.

But I also had some "friends" who wouldn't let me in their makeup circle. They would attend outside classes and wouldn't invite me. They would host classes and wouldn't tell me until the very last minute because they knew that I couldn't come up with the money that they were charging that quickly.

I remember there was one makeup artist that I wanted to see—Maree Antoinette. Every time there was an opportunity to see her, either I wasn't told until the last minute or I couldn't afford it.

That same year, a makeup artist, Kevin Kirk, was preparing for his annual Jam Session event. Kevin was visiting salons promoting Jam Session and when I found out that this other makeup artist was going to be educating at Jam Session, I bought that ticket so fast and then I reached out to her to see if there was any way that I could help her.

I helped her find models for the event and I was so excited to see her teach the class, but I never could have imagined what God had in store for me that night that was going to change the direction of my life.

※

I was sitting in her class soaking up all of the wisdom that she had to share when I felt a tap on my shoulder. I looked to answer and the young lady said, "Tanya would like to see you!"

I was like, who me? How does Tanya know me? I thought to myself. So I followed the young lady to the prep area and Tanya said, "Are you Alarice's cousin who does makeup?"

Coolly, I responded, "Yes."

Her son went to the prom with my cousin's daughter and I did her makeup for the prom that year. Tanya replied, "Can you help us tonight? Our makeup artist didn't show up and we need someone to do our models' makeup." Unfortunately, I didn't have my makeup bag so I told her that I couldn't do it.

I went back into the makeup class and sat next to my friend Ki. I told her what had just happened.

She looked at me and said, "Girl if you don't get your tail up and go home and get that bag, you don't know what God is trying to do!"

So I did just that. I got up and went back into the prep room and told Tanya that I was going home to get the bag and that I was coming right back. I came back and did their makeup for the team.

Kevin and Tanya were major heavy hitters, so it was a pleasant surprise that they were very pleased with my work (which I was glad about because they both intimidated me, lol).

✴

That night marked a new beginning. After a successful night, Kevin and Tanya asked me to travel to the Bronner Brothers show with them and become their makeup artist and I have been traveling with them as their Lead Makeup Artist ever since!

I believe that connecting with Kevin totally changed the direction that my life was going in my profession. That opportunity began to rebuild my confidence in addition to helping me find my niche in the industry.

Because I was his makeup artist I have had the chance to work and travel with reputable companies such as Babyliss Pro and Rusk. I served the Kirk Pro brand as their lead makeup artist for two Bronner Brothers wins.

I present as an educator for Jam Session and I educate for other makeup conferences as well. I even went back and got my cosmetology instructor's license, which has afforded me the position of Cosmetology Instructor for the High School in my city.

✴

Connecting to Kevin gave me the desire to be healthy as well. Remember I said that I had found the weight that I lost and then some, right? Whew!!! I was reaching for 300 lbs at my heaviest.

I remember during my divorce process, my Pastor lead our church on a 21-day fast. I had started traveling with the KirkPro team and still serving on the worship team at church and it had all become very taxing on my body. And that was because of my weight. I was so overweight, I had to take my heels off and wear flats to sing, I couldn't carry that weight and sing at the same time.

One of my prayers during that time was that God would help me lose weight because I couldn't do the work He called me to do carrying that extra weight on my body. Once the 21-day fast was over, I had honestly forgotten the prayer I prayed! I went back to eating what I had been eating before the fast.

Two weeks later, something in my mind clicked, I had a strong desire to change my way of eating. I began to eat a low carb diet and I reached out to Fitness Trainer, Crystal Andrea, to start training.

I remember joking with Kevin that I looked at my fellow teammates and knew I needed to get sexy to be on his team, which got me down an even 90 lbs… Dig that!

☀

I now help other women (and men) lose weight through my own experience. I help them with meal plans and workouts, and I even became a certified Zumba Instructor.

God has even given me the opportunity to help other women that are going through divorce. Some of these women are old enough to be my mother, but they trust me because they watched me walk through a tough place and make it through.

I am able to be the trauma nurse for these women that my trauma nurses were for me. I have even been invited to come speak about my divorce experience on different platforms. But the most beautiful thing that God did was heal my friendship with my ex-husband. The marriage may be over, but he is still one of my closest friends and there is nothing but love and respect between us.

And his son is my favorite little buddy. He is the sweetest, cutest, smartest, happiest, most intelligent little man in the world, and I absolutely love him.

Sometimes the things that the enemy tried to use to hurt you, God will use that same thing to heal you. God had a plan for my pain and my life… Kevin has been the driving force and major inspiration that has pushed me to the next stage in my career.

On this journey, I rediscovered my love for Makeup and for Myself.

To watch the LIVE taping of the Behind the Scenes Interview with Kevin Kirk and other beauty experts, go to **bit.ly/beastinthebeauty**

Password Required: beast2020 (case sensitive)

des ·tine

\\ˈde-stən\\

to decree beforehand; predetermine

style 6

Depressed Yet Not Defeated

Sherlisa Walker

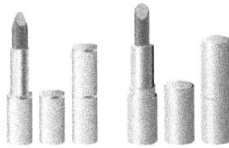

Diamond stood in her stockroom. Her breath was shallow yet still strong. Everyone thought she had it made, but inside, she was miserable. How did she end up here? For years, she loved what she did. Now she felt trapped in her job and lost without any real sense of fulfillment.

She worked here going on five years. She realized she never worked anywhere for longer than five years. What happened to her dreams? More so than that, what happened to her home life? Her time with her children? Her time, dedication, and commitment to her church home? Everything seemed wrong…

Her eyes filled with tears, and her chest rose and fell from her deep inhaling. She wanted to leave to live out her purpose. She didn't know when she lost sight of that fact, but she longed for more.

☀

Diamond was fifteen when she first dreamed of becoming a hairstylist. Her interest in this field peaked when she spent summers away in Houston, TX. Her cousin Angie often coiffed her hair in the latest styles known to the coolest rappers.

One hot Saturday back in '91, she sat while Angie cut and styled the freshest stack hairstyle on her. Her hair was smooth, cool, and exactly like Pepa from the popular group Salt N Pepa. She couldn't wait for school back home in Wacto, TX to start so she could show all her friends.

☀

Man, what a weekend, Diamond thought to herself. Monday came, time for her to return to work. Saturday's sales put her store on top. They kept heavy foot traffic, but she and her staff floated throughout the store racking up sales. They moved swiftly, determined to please each customer who entered the gate.

She came in early to call her District Manager, Mr. Stormy Easterling, to inform him of her plans to resign. She planned to call before the store opened but after arriving, she changed her mind. At 10:00 a.m., she opened the gate to her store.

The store had been open for several hours and each time the phone rang, her stomach knotted. Around the fifth call, she picked up the phone and heard his voice on the line. He called to discuss the results of the weekend's sales. Before she realized it, Diamond blurted out her desire to part ways.

To her surprise, Mr. Easterling asked where she would work, and why she would want to leave her current position with no real sense of security. She didn't have any more of a clue as to what she would do than he did. She was confident her time at Lady Footlocker had come to an end.

In the back of her mind, she remembered an old friend gave her a lead for a job—it was for a position as a Certified Nursing Assistant (CNA) at the hospital across town three days a week. After Diamond hung up the phone, she began to research her options.

By the end of the week, Diamond was confident she had all the answers she needed. It was time to start the next stage of her life. She set up an interview at the hospital her friend mentioned to her. Everything seemed to be falling in line, she knew she made the right decision to give her resignation.

The healthcare field proved to be a lot more strenuous than Diamond ever imagined. This was her first position as a Certified Nursing Assistant. She never understood the magnitude of what they go through and experience each and every day.

Diamond didn't mind working twelve-hour shifts. She conditioned herself for long hours in her previous career choices. The problem came in when she had to learn to work with and care for many patients at one time. The patient-to-aide ratio was so broad. She found herself caring for up to eighteen patients consecutively. Some of them needed to be fed. Many of them needed to be changed. Others needed her help in and out of bed. Yet all of the patients needed bathing. It was somewhat of a relief if they refused to eat or bathe.

With the heavy work schedule, Diamond enrolled in an online two-year college course. She also planned to take her Cosmetology exam in Texas. Luckily, after all these years, her hours in Texas did not expire. She thanked God for this because she couldn't afford to pay for cosmetology school. She needed her license to one day operate a successful business.

☼

A former instructor gave Diamond a mock practical examination pamphlet. She also found an updated version online and printed it. She concentrated on each section from the pamphlets. Three months later she decided to apply for the exam. It had been two decades since she attended beauty school. She planned to take the test and see which area she would need to improve on before getting licensed.

She and her best friend at the time, Marina, drove to Plano, Texas where they stayed at the Nylo Hotel. Some decor needed remodeling but it was still a comfortable and clean place to stay. The breakfast was to die for, and she dreamed of one day hosting a business event in their media center. She needed to unwind and calm her nerves the night before the exam.

The following morning Diamond's nerves were all over the place. She showered, got dressed, and grabbed her bag with the supplies and instruments she would need to take the exam.

Marina drove to the testing site. They both sat without talking in their rental car until the doors opened. She and Marina joined hands and said a quick prayer. Oddly enough, the nervousness disappeared. She laughed to herself because that was definitely not the case the first time she took the exam. The first time, she was a nervous wreck and failed the exam. This time, she was more than ready.

☀

Diamond presented her driver's license and information packet with her testing ID number. The examination room was as she expected... there were mirrors everywhere. She stood confident about executing each section of the exam even though she didn't know if she'd pass the test. Who cared if she did or not? She wanted the learning experience, and she took the challenge.

Diamond looked around, uncomfortable with her outfit. The last time she checked the dress code still required those taking the exam to wear all white. A white shirt, white pants, white shoes, and a white smock. One of the ladies next to her had on a gray and black outfit that resembled a warm-up suit. She felt out of place and much older than everyone in the room.

Everyone took a seat while the proctors tallied the scores. In years past, she waited for her results in the mail. An open discussion began and a proctor stated how impressed she was with how Diamond dressed. She said it reminded her of how everyone dressed for their test back in her day. She smiled at the proctor with gratitude.

A few moments later the room got quiet. The test results were ready. Diamond glanced around the room and noticed that everyone else seemed nervous. She stayed at ease. She reminded herself she only wanted to familiarize herself with the exam. She already planned to return and ace it on her next visit. She took her envelope and walked towards the exit door with her used examination kit in tow.

In the hallway, she mustered up enough courage to open the envelope to look at her test score. How could this be?

She didn't believe her eyes. This can't be right she thought to herself. Did someone make a mistake? Then reality set in as she glanced up at her name and operator number at the top of the piece of paper. A huge smile broke out on her face as she realized she passed the exam. She was now a licensed cosmetologist. She picked up her kit, threw it over her shoulder and thought to herself, "Now that's Gangsta..."

☀

Not long after she received her cosmetology license in Texas, Diamond took the reciprocity exam in Arkansas. That test only consisted of multiple-choice questions. Once again, she received her score before she left the testing site. As soon as she received the news that she passed, she called her friend J'Wanna and informed her. Not too many days later, J'Wanna hired her.

Diamond accepted a nail tech position at Serenity Nail Spa. She loved the location and understood she now worked in one of the best neighborhoods in the city. The clientele rocked. The atmosphere and the commute were good. Everything seemed perfect, that is until she found it hard to work on complete strangers.

She serviced her friends and regular clients with ease. Strangers were another story altogether. They sensed she didn't have much experience. Months passed, she got better but never completely comfortable.

She stayed employed at Serenity Nail Spa until she decided to venture out on her own as a salon owner. For a while, she heard of Sola Salons. This new concept offered multiple suites housed under the same roof. Each stylist owned their Salon and ran their business the way they saw fit. She figured she would look further into this type of business structure. She called the owner, met with him, and before long, she owned a salon!

☀

Diamond loved to be able to unlock and open the door to her business. She was confident she made the right choice. She made a deal with the owner that it would be two to three weeks before she would launch her salon. It still felt good to go in and map out how she would set things up and how she would plan her day.

She also decided she would offer one-on-one classes to train on methods and procedures not generally offered in beauty schools. Now that she earned her license, she didn't want to see anyone else have to go through years of frustration. Her classes would help to build confidence in their skills and learn how to sustain themselves in order to build their careers so that they could feed their families and not give up on their dreams.

☀

Shortly after signing the lease to her Salon, Diamond realized the annual Bronner Brothers show started in a few weeks and started making plans to attend. She invited her niece Rebecca and her children's father, Legend, to attend. Her niece completed beauty school, but she never decided to take the exam. Her children's father attended cosmetology school but chose to go a different route and registered for barber school. In her mind, the trip would be a motivation for the three of them. She wanted to take some educational classes for herself and add to her teaching skills. Both Rebecca and Legend agreed to attend, and they set a date to set out on their journey.

It took quite a while to make it from Arkansas to Atlanta, but they had a ball on the car ride. They sang and talked and started making plans on how they would spend their weekend. Diamond was the only one who attended before, so she tried her best to inform them both of what to expect. In years past the Bronner Brothers shows were always the highlight of her year whenever she attended. Little did she know, this would be the first of many trips that would no longer bring her such joy.

※

They arrived at the Omni Hotel, relieved to finally reach their destination. A valet driver walked up to the car, and they began to pile out of the car one by one. Excited and eager, Diamond hopped out of the passenger side. She walked right into the approaching valet driver and dropped her phone on the pavement. It completely shattered. She wondered how she would complete her homework being that she left her laptop at home. She thought to herself, "I'll worry about that later."

They checked in, unpacked, and walked over to the Georgia World Congress Center. Diamond made her first major buy, a Golden Supreme Marcel stove and iron set. The combination of a hot pink and a cooler tone of the shade like the color of Pepto Bismol. Pink was her favorite color and it was an item she dreamed of owning since beauty school. She and Rebecca also purchased 'I Work Too Hard Boo' t-shirts designed by one of Atlanta's hottest hairstylists. They even managed to take a pic with her. They loved how pleasant and inviting she was as celebrities are not always so cool.

Afterward, they headed out to find Legend who made a few purchases of his own. He secured a new clipper set, smock, clipper combs, and a carrying bag for all his items. All three were hungry by this point and returned to their hotel room to drop off their purchases. Immediately they walked over to the CNN Center. They discussed how and when to navigate the Congress Center to get the most out of the show. They finished up their meals and headed back over towards the Congress Center.

Hours later they returned to their room. They scrapped their earlier plan to hit up the local strip club. After a long day of walking and sightseeing, they decided to call it a night.

☀

The next morning they got up, got dressed, and again walked back over to the Congress center. The exhibit floor had people everywhere. This time around they mapped out all the classes they wanted to attend and begin to go their separate ways. For the most part, Rebecca and Diamond attended the same classes. Legend attended classes that catered to barbers.

☀

Diamond was happy for Legend because for the first time in years he had a glow in his spirit. For nine years she watched as his anger grew with himself, those around him, and life in general. She remembered the day things started to change as if it happened yesterday.

Diamond would never forget August 29, 2004. At the time they only owned one operating vehicle. She worked at Dallas/Fort Worth International airport as a group red supervisor. Legend worked at the Roomstore as a field manager. He visited stores in his district to set up displays and take pictures. His stepdad also worked at the airport and Diamond would sometimes catch a ride home with him. Legend's mother would keep the children while both of them worked.

This particular day Diamond rode home with Legend's step dad to his and his wife's apartment. Legend would be getting off work in three hours. Unbeknownst to Diamond or anyone else, their lives were about to change.

The local police department knocked on the door. His mother answered and the policeman stepped inside the apartment. The officer asked if she knew Legend L. Evans. Somewhat hesitant to answer she confirmed indeed she did. First, he apologized. Then he informed her that Legend was in an accident. They airlifted him to a hospital in Dallas, at least 20 minutes away from Arlington.

Immediately Diamond's heart sank as she looked at her babies and collapsed on the floor. She opened her eyes and realized she had been crying so hard she drooled all over the carpet. She composed herself. Her children were nervous and afraid. Legend's dad started to gather everyone and urged them down to the car. Her eldest son could not stop crying. He only wanted to see his dad. No matter how hard she tried to comfort him, he screamed and cried all the way to the hospital. Her youngest son wept, but he didn't quite understand.

It seemed as if it took several days for them to reach the hospital. A nurse guided them to step into a family room to speak with a Chaplin. Diamond knew this was not good. Either Legend died or he was bad off with little hope of survival? A cold chill settled over her body as the Chaplin did his best to prepare them to go into the room. But she couldn't help but think that Chaplins are called when someone has either died or not expected to recover. Question was: which was Legend?

☀

Legend's face looked gray and had swollen at least five times the size of his normal face. His misshapen ankle reminded her of an elephant's foot. Tubes came out of his body in every direction. The tube in his throat pumped air in and out of his body. She didn't know how to feel. The thought and the pain of losing her other half threatened to be a reality.

There were problems, but at this moment she didn't know what she would do without him. It was as if she lost part of her soul. What about their babies? What would they do without their dad? He couldn't leave now. They had so much more life to live. She prayed that he would live. No matter what they went through she convinced herself that none of that mattered. She loved him and she would stick by his side.

Those memories were always etched deep in the back of her mind. Even though she would never forget, her mind stayed on her budding business.

☀

The three of them met up for lunch to discuss the classes they attended. Once back on the exhibit floor, Diamond loaded up on a few more Nairobi products. The Bronner Brothers show always offered package deals. Vendors sold awesome packages for her own personal needs. She could also resell to her clients. Life was always a win-win for her. They did more sightseeing and networking and then retired to their room.

Diamond remembered she needed to turn in her homework. All assignments had to be in by midnight on Sunday. She still had work to do. That's when it hit her. She shattered her phone. With her laptop back home she needed to find a solution. She turned to Legend, woke him up and asked to use his phone for her studies. He handed it to her, and she logged into her student account. A few hours later, she submitted all her assignments and let out a huge sigh of relief.

It dawned on her that she didn't check her social media sites the entire weekend. Being that she had Legend's phone, she would have to log out of his account and then log into hers. As she started to log out, she caught on that Legend had a multitude of female friends. She tried to ignore the feeling but then something didn't sit right with her. She started to open some messages.

Some iffy ones, but nothing stuck out as odd. At least not in any of the messages she opened. At some point, something urged her to look at his friend list on the book of many faces. He friended so many females she couldn't keep count. She opened his messages and again she was uneasy. She scrolled up and down the list, and she couldn't point it out but the feeling wouldn't leave her alone. At first glance, nothing seemed out of place. She continued to look and thought to herself, "I need to stop because I am tripping."

After checking a few more messages, Diamond started to feel bad about assuming he was foul. She started to log out and that same urge told her to reopen the messages. She scrolled higher and there it was. Right in his messages, staring her dead in the face. The words flew off of the screen and slapped her right upside her head. Her intuition never failed. She reminded herself that things between them had been so strained. They lived apart as much time as they spent together. But this time, they said they would tough it out together.

She sat there trying to process what she read. During one of the times they were together and everything was smooth, Legend had an affair. His sister referred to the girl as their cousin. Now she realized why he would get upset when she would refer to Tina as his cousin. He would always reply, "Tina ain't my damn cousin."

Shouldn't she have realized it then? She never considered Tina to be attractive, nor did she believe Tina to be Legend's type. On top of that, she knew men passed that girl around more times than mashed potatoes on Thanksgiving. Diamond remembered how Legend's own friends would make passes at the girl. She knew from hanging out with her, Tina rarely passed up offers.

Her heart sank deeper and deeper. She moved on and opened more messages where he interacted with several other females. A few of them showed how heartless Legend had become when it came to his loyalty towards Diamond. She wanted to confront him. If she didn't have any proof he would once again lie and say she made up the whole thing. She couldn't send the messages to her phone because it wouldn't even hold a charge. She sat there for a moment then figured she would wake Rebecca.

As Rebecca looked up Diamond said, "I hate to place you in our business. I know if I don't have a witness he will lie and say I'm making up this shit." Rebecca was reluctant but took the phone and looked through the messages. When she finished, she let out a quick sigh.

Diamond pulled out the mini cups of alcohol they purchased. Before long, she drank sixteen. She was so mellow and polite when she woke Legend up and asked him to follow her out onto the balcony. Confused, he said in a soft low tone, "Baby what's wrong?" Diamond replied, "Step outside let me talk to you."

As soon as they both were far enough out Diamond turned to Legend and stated, "I don't want to fight. I don't want to argue. When we get back, I need you to get whatever shit you have at my place and get the fuck out of my house."

Legend immediately started to panic, still unsure of what exactly happened. As she started to walk away Legend grabbed Diamond by the arm and said, "Wait, baby, why? Look at me. What's wrong? What happened?"

Diamond responded, "Why don't you ask that bitch Tina what happened?" Legend immediately dropped his head.

For her, that was all the proof Diamond needed. That and she read for herself how the two engaged in a long and deceitful affair. She thought of the many times she applied lashes on the tramp. Her children played with his mistresses' children. She always wondered why when they went to family night on Sundays, Tina would show up with her children and no man. Could it be that all along, her man was Tina's man too?

☼

Emotions told her to go and walk through the city. The sight of Legend angered her, and she needed to be alone. By this time they were back into the room so Diamond got dressed to leave. From their hotel room, they could see the famous Ferris wheel of Atlanta. She decided she would figure out how to go there, then remembered her broken phone. She couldn't take the chance on getting lost in a city she was not too familiar with outside of the Congress Center. Where would she go without a destination and no GPS to help her navigate?

As she plopped down on the bed tension started to build, so she decided to start packing up her luggage. She and Legend exchanged words. He wouldn't open his phone for them to read the messages together. In true fashion as before, he denied anything had happened but this time she had proof. She read it. As she watched him sit in the chair across from her, he had the audacity to begin to erase messages from his phone. She was mad as hell.

She looked at the blanket and pillow set Legend gave her during one of their better times together. Grabbing both pieces, she tossed them into the trash. "I no longer need this shit."

Legend got up to retrieve the items and as she glared at him she saw the first signs of remorse she had ever seen on his face. It didn't faze her but it saddened her to see him react like that over a damn pillow and blanket set.

Frustration replaced any remorse upon his face. The argument continued and got more and more intense. He knocked over her jewelry bag and in the process, broke one of her favorite necklaces. She confronted him, and he drew back to swing on her. She yelled what are you going to do, hit me? Embarrassed by his actions and the thought of his niece watching, he dropped his hand and walked away. Diamond finished packing her bags. She and Rebecca shared a bed that night as she drifted off to sleep.

☀

When Diamond awakened, thoughts of the night before filled her head. For so long she had been so strong. She had been everyone else's support system. Now she couldn't even muster up the strength to stand. She laid in bed long enough for the tears to begin to well up in her eyes. But before a single tear dropped she blinked them away. Rebecca was already awake, applying makeup and getting dressed.

Their conversation was light and Rebecca tried her best to brighten the mood. Diamond went along with the jokes because she didn't want to think about her problems. Legend got dressed by his bed, and they all walked back over to the Congress center together.

Diamond purchased a few more items for her daughter and her shop and waited on her two companions. After shopping, they returned to the hotel and gathered all their belongings and headed downstairs to check out the room.

The Front Desk attendant looked at her face and asked if everything was okay. With tears already streaming down her face, Diamond replied, "I'm fine except that I found out my kids' father cheated on me with someone I viewed as a friend."

The attendant stretched out her hand and grasped Diamond's. She said she would pray for her then released her hand and handed her a tissue. Diamond thanked her. She placed her sunglasses on her face and followed Rebecca and Legend into the elevator. A few minutes later they were back inside the parking garage. Only this time everyone understood this would be a much longer ride.

The only noise came from the radio. As bad as Diamond tried to hold it all in, tears continued to flow down her cheeks. She was usually filled with joy and optimism. The sad and unhappy emotions were not familiar in her world. She recently lost her father. If he was alive, she could cope much better.

With her father gone, she no longer had her confidante to turn to when life hit her hard. He always reassured her. He would have the answer to whatever problem she faced. She recalled growing up thinking she was a real-life princess. An incident at school clued her in that she was a normal little girl like everyone else. Yet, because of the way her father treated her, she continued to live like royalty. Now here she is next to a man who didn't know her worth, let alone his own.

☼

As the hours passed and the miles flew by Diamond became more and more heated. Her mind couldn't understand how she ended up here. She questioned Legend, and he continued to try to change the subject. Hurt and irritated, she finally gave up her fight.

At some point, Legend's eldest sister called and told her not to worry. She said Legend loved her, but that men will be men. There was history and three beautiful children that loved them. Diamond wanted to believe it but her heart and mind couldn't conceive what she heard. Who in the world cared about history and whether someone claimed to love you? True love shouldn't hurt and history meant nothing if it was full of lies.

She didn't know how she could continue to trust Legend. She could never continue to love someone she couldn't trust. Besides what was up with the comment that men will be men? What if 'men being men' occurred because that's what the women allowed? Maybe men would not be able to do so if women held them to certain standards.

By the time they made it back to Arkansas, Diamond stopped trying to understand. How ironic that she wanted Legend to attend the show with her? She thought they could mend their relationship and build a business together. In three days her entire plan had failed.

☀

Diamond fought hard to make it through the next week. The weekend left her with little energy. She cared for others, but she needed someone to care for her. Time passed faster than she expected but it still seemed to take forever for her days to end. Thursday she worked at the hospital and Sunday she attended church. She couldn't tell a single soul what the pastor preached about that day. The next Monday seemed to fare better as she booked her day to capacity, and thus her slow and lengthy healing took form.

The next few months challenged Diamond. Inside, she was empty. Business at the shop took off. That is, whenever she had the strength to show up to work. Some days she couldn't force herself to be in the shop. On the days she could, she would try her best to stack her clients.

Things were much different at the hospital. She had no choice but to interact with others. To her coworkers and regular patients, not much had changed. She remained upbeat and willing to help whomever. There were times she could be short but that was a given in her line of work. Her job duties were so intense some days that it was easy for anyone to get overwhelmed. Many days she went through the motions.

☀

For months on end, she would leave work, go home, and drink until she hardly felt anything except sleep. Her children would knock on her door and call her phone. She would lie there and not respond unless she had to feed them, help with homework, or bath time for her daughter. Other than that, she laid emotionless.

She had a problem, but she couldn't pull herself together. She needed help but chose not to seek it. How could it be that she helped others solve their issues but couldn't help herself? She was the one everyone depended on for answers. She wondered if they knew her story, how many would stop calling? It didn't matter anyway. All she could do was pray. Pray that things would change. Pray that the hurt would go away. Prayer would give her the strength to be strong again.

☀

Month after month Diamond felt more stressed than depressed. She wanted to feel like herself again, but she still suffered unrelenting anxiety. She couldn't take the thought of being with or around Legend. At the same time, she was sad that their relationship was at a definite end.

So many times they broke up and got back together. Somehow, someway they always found their way back to each other. This time felt different. All the stress caused her severe stomach pains. She could hardly eat anything without being sick. Sometimes the smell of food made her ill. Whenever she did eat, she couldn't keep much down without vomiting.

One evening Legend called and Diamond explained her issue to him. He decided he'd take her to a doctor, and she called the next morning to make the appointment. The doctor diagnosis was irritable bowel syndrome. Her esophagus nearly closed due to acid buildup. The doctor told her she almost came in too late. The opening was about the size of a nickel. They scheduled an appointment to have her esophagus dilated.

Legend drove her and after the procedure, they stopped to eat. The procedure hurt her throat and made it hard to swallow. She went home to rest and Legend helped her to bed. He slept on her couch and checked on her throughout the night. Hours later, she awakened to her daughter sleeping at her side. She got up and walked into the bathroom then into the living room to find Legend already awake. She found herself kissing him. She couldn't tell if he kissed her, or she kissed him, but she liked it.

But, how could she? Why would she? Moments later she found herself thanking God for restoring her family. It took time for them to work things out and Legend gave her an engagement ring. The wedding plans started and they were happy with each other again.

✵

Marriage never topped Diamond's list. She didn't have fantasies about her wedding day. Her dreams consisted of her being a career woman with a luxury vehicle and her own business. A beautiful home complete with the white picket fence completed the picture.

Three children, and a fiancé later, and her outlook on marriage had changed. She had asked several of her closest friends, her niece and goddaughter to be her bridesmaids. A handful of them accompanied her to David's Bridal to buy bridesmaid dresses together.

Legend and Diamond wanted to get married on the anniversary of his accident. It would turn an unhappy memory into the best day of their lives. They only had six months to pull everything together. They secured her church home for the venue. They even found a cute little spot to have the reception and serve alcohol. Her nerves were on edge but there was still no one else with whom she wanted to share her life.

✵

Now, as Diamond settled into her career, severe stomach pains returned. She found herself succumbed to her bed more and once again becoming bed-bound. Exhausted, one day she picked up the phone and called Martin, the owner of her salon suites to discontinue her room rental for her salon. She explained her health situation to him and he completely understood. He informed her that he was sad about her situation and if she ever wanted to come back and rent again, she would be welcome to if space allowed.

On the day she removed all her belongings, she met with Martin to turn in her key. It hurt to feel as if she gave up on her dream. She thanked him and went on her way.

※

Diamond continued to make wedding plans and even those started to fall apart. First, it was Legend's dad who couldn't attend. He was in recovery from surgery. Next, it was her Aunt who had back problems and needed surgery. Then it was her Uncle who had issues at home. He was the primary caretaker of his children after his wife passed away. There was no way she would get married without her dad's siblings there to witness. Her dad was gone. Not having them there would devastate her. To her, there was no way she could go through with their plans without having her father or the most important people in her life there with her on her special day. It just wouldn't be right.

Discussing this with Legend proved to be a task. To him, he could only hear that she didn't want to marry him. That was farthest from the truth. Even though marriage was never her top priority, she felt like the luckiest woman alive when he asked her to be his wife. It was just the circumstances surrounding them that made her feel like they should wait a while before they went through with the wedding.

No matter what was said, Legend just could not understand. Their relationship became more strained than ever and Legend started to distance himself from her. Diamond began to feel lonely and alone and they both started hanging out with friends separately.

During that time Diamond decided to focus on her business. One night she met another business owner at a meeting for a possible business opportunity and they became friends. They didn't hang out much, but they talked on the phone about business plans and possibly helping each other build their businesses.

Eventually, business guy started to express an interest in Diamond. She knew it was wrong, but with her now feeling lonely, fat, old, and unwanted, she in turn continued to entertain his advances. Nothing sexual occurred, a few texts were sent here and there. They were filled with details of what he planned to do with and to her, but she was merely going along with it to make herself feel better.

Somehow her heart still belonged to Legend. Her depression kicked in even stronger at this point because she truly felt lost without him, yet she knew things would quite possibly never be the same. Before long, she her feelings for Legend became numb. She started to not care about his whereabouts and they drifted further and further apart. It was as if they were together, but still so far apart. She suspected he felt pretty much the same about her.

One day, out of the blue, Legend walked into Diamond's bedroom. She jumped from the force of the door opening, then for some reason she placed her phone underneath her leg. At that point, she had nothing to hide. She hadn't even talked to the business guy.

Legend noticed and got his hands on her phone. Once he unlocked the screen, he began scrolling through the phone as if he was looking for something in particular. A few minutes later, he discovered the texts from the business guy.

Hell it had been months since she had talked to him! Although her relationship with Legend had still been strained, she no longer felt the need to be entertained by the business guy, so she cut it off. Oh but there was no way she could explain that to Legend! He was definitely not having it. He became even more short and distant. This had definitely taken a turn in the wrong direction.

For months and months on end, the communication between the two was barely existent. Diamond couldn't help but feel she had single-handedly torn apart her family. More importantly, she felt she had let her children down. They no longer saw their mother in the same light. All of this occurred because she was selfish in wanting to feel like someone cared.

She asked herself over and over again *why would she allow herself to be so weak.* For her, she was never one of those women who felt they couldn't live without a man. Of course she understood having a partner was a bonus, but she knew she could live without one. *So why was she so stuck on Legend?*

They both had done wrong but her heart still ached for him. It didn't matter anyway because she would never let him know. She knew the best way to deal with her emotions was to dismiss them and to come off unconcerned. Whenever they did have conversations, Legend would often remind her of her little friend Ray Allison, and that maybe she should discuss things with him.

Things had really gotten bad. Before long, Legend found someone to entertain himself. This was much different than Diamond's situation. She knew that he more than likely was attracted to the person he was conversing with. At first, she was only angered and decided that things should end. Then she became confused and realized that she might loose him forever. This made the state of their relationship seem so real.

She found herself crying. This hurt more than she ever thought it would and it caused her deep pain. That same pain forced her to take a deep look within. She came to the realization that she, too, played a huge part in the breakdown of their union.

For so long she always thought things weren't going smoothly because Legend could not get it right. Hell, now she knew SHE couldn't get it right either! From those belittling conversations to dismissing his presence all together, they taught each other how not to fight for the one you loved.

Truth be told, she had become so angry and resentful that she wasn't always too kind. She was so focused on being strong and not taking "no shit" from anyone; that she would shut herself out and turn away from him whenever she felt he had hurt her.

Yeah, she had a tough exterior most times and she kept it that way, at least up until the end. She never imagined the hurt she would feel if she lost him forever—outside of when she almost lost him from the car accident. Being seen as weak was the least of her worries now.

Boldly speaking, losing him now hurt her just as much as it did when she almost lost him all those years ago. Diamond knew she had to be strong and she knew she had to be strong quick. She now understood the choices we make and the things we allow in life can make you so hateful. She also now understood Legend was not the only one who needed to get better. She needed help as well. She then told herself, "Sometimes it ain't always him, Sis..... sometimes it's you, too girl....."

Diamond's story to be continued...

About the
Authors

Kevin Kirk

Co-Lead Author

Kevin Kirk is a native of Bessemer, Alabama and a graduate of Hueytown High School and Step Ahead Cosmetology School. Kevin is the Chief Executive Officer of KirkPro, founded in 2012 to provide the hair care industry with new and innovative products for multicultural hair care.

Kevin is currently one of the founding members of the Babybliss Pro Artistic Team and is the current Team Leader/Artistic Director. He is the founder of Hair Artistry Jam Session, an annual networking and educational event for hair care and beauty industry professionals and students. He is also the former Rusk Deepshine Pure Pigment Conditioning Cream Color Educator, working directly with Salon Center.

Kevin has been competing on the national level for several years and some of his greatest accomplishments are winning Bronner Brothers' International Hair Battle four times, the only competitor in Bronner Brothers history to do so. In 2017, Kevin won the 70th Anniversary Bronner Brothers' Hair Battle in Atlanta with a breathtaking aerial performance titled, "Beauty for Ashes"!

His other wins include Bronners Brothers Houston, Atlanta 2009, and the $50,000 Hair Battle Royale in Baltimore.

Kevin has been featured in issues of Upscale magazine, Matrix magazine, Hype Hair magazine, The Source magazine, Modern Salon, and other nationally distributed publications.

He has also appeared in two national reality television programs, "Ambushed Make Over" and "Tears, Shears, & Beauty". He co-starred, along with Chris Rock, in the HBO movie titled "Good Hair". "Good Hair" is a documentary film about African-American hair stylists, hair styles, and the roles they have in African-American culture.

Kevin's work has also been featured on CNN's website. Kevin appeared, competed, and won The Look All Star competition, a national reality tv show where the top beauty industry leaders compete against one another. Kevin recently won Bronner Bros. Icon Award Educators of the Year.

Kevin is committed to using his God-given vision and artistic talents to change the hair care landscape as we know it, and to leave an international legacy that will be unmatched for generations to come.

Mark 11:23-24 (KJV)

[23]For verily I say unto you, That whosoever shall say unto this mountain, Be thou removed, and be thou cast into the sea; and shall not doubt in his heart, but shall believe that those things which he saith shall come to pass; he shall have whatsoever he saith. [24]Therefore I say unto you, What things soever ye desire, when ye pray, believe that ye receive them, and ye shall have them.

Find Kevin online at kevinkirkpro.com

Social Media handle: @kevinkirk1

Vicki Kirk May

Co-Lead Author

Vicki Kirk May is a 23-year-veteran educator in the State of Alabama. Vicki has received numerous degrees in Elementary education with Honors. Because she is a life-long learner, she seeks out opportunities to stay on top of the latest and most effective ways of teaching children. With all that she has accomplished, her biggest accomplishment is her family.

Being a wife, mother, grandmother, daughter, elder, and ordained minister of the Gospel is true success to Vicki. She is driven by her passion and purpose to change the lives of children one teacher at a time.

Known as the Educator's Passion Accelerator, Vicki believes that we all are endowed with gifts and passions to make the world better. Those gifts should not be bound by fear, mediocrity, or status quo, but unleashed to effectuate change in the world and lead you to a life experienced by overflow and abundance.

Realizing that a disruption in education had to take place in order for evolution to occur, Vicki set out on her entrepreneurial journey. Vicki provides personal and professional development for educators who are ready to go to the next level in their careers and personal life by becoming the best and highest versions of who they really be.

She is an award winning author, speaker, and consultant. Vicki travels the nation showing educators and entrepreneurs how to become great leaders by becoming the highest version of themselves through leadership training, seminars, retreats, and live events.

She is the founder of the National Teachers Support Network, an organization created to provide a safe judgment-free community of support for teachers to connect personally, professionally, and socially. NTSN acts as a conduit for educators to receive the support necessary to become the best version of themselves. The mission of NTSN is to equip and empower teachers with the resources, skills, and knowledge necessary to experience their best life in and out of the classroom. For further information about becoming a part of NTSN, go to nationalteacherssupportnetwork.org.

Jennifer Bowens
Co-Author

Jennifer "JB Nicole" Bowens has always had a passion for doing hair. She learned how to braid at an early age of 6. Being from a small town didn't stop her from wanting BIG things! Having overcome many obstacles, JB still worked hard to withstand entrepreneurship and life, and learning to evolve in an industry that's slowly becoming diverse.

In the past years, JB Nicole has challenged herself to grow by focusing on education. She is not only a Master Cosmetologist and Cosmetology Instructor, she also has certifications in Hair Loss and Non-Surgical Hair Replacement, Wig Making, Multi-textural Locking techniques, and Numerous Hair Extension Techniques.

JB Nicole also has her own product line, Miss J's Growth Oil, that she hopes to expand in the future. She has been a salon owner for almost 10 years and plans on opening a new Hair Loss Center in the next two years.

Ashley Michelle Hawkins
Co-Author

Born and raised in Florence, South Carolina, AshleyMichelle is a cosmetologist and entrepreneur who started her hair care journey in 2014. She always knew she wanted to use her skills to give back to her community.

In 2018, AshleyMichelle was licensed upon completion of Kenneth Schuler School of Cosmetology. Soon after, she worked at local beauty shop, Kutz N Kurlz; and only months later, started AshleyMichelle LLC. AshleyMichelle currently provides beauty services and event planning, with plans to add personalized wigs, bundles, eyelashes and more to her portfolio.

After hosting her own fashion and hair show in November 2019, AsheyMichelle launched her own denim line. AshleyMichelle does not only do hair, but she strives to take care of her community with her *Giving Back Confidence* event where she provides free hair and skin care services to the local shelter.

Erika Nicole Lawson King
Co-Author

Erika Lawson King is the owner of Esteem Beauty Studios and proprietor of Erika Nicole Artistry. As lead make-up artist for Kirk Pro (the product line for international, award-winning stylist, Kevin Kirk); freelance makeup artist for Smashbox and MAC, and Licensed Cosmetologist Instructor at Bessemer City High School, she is the personification of a multi-dimensional entrepreneur.

Enduring many challenges, setbacks and heartbreaks in her own life has only motivated her to adopt the philosophy of Philippians 2:3, "Let nothing be done through strife or vainglory; but in lowliness (humbleness) of mind let each esteem other better than themselves."

Erika endeavors to create an environment unlike the usual competitive and sometimes "mean" intents of society, especially among women. Instead, she helps to transform lives by first uncovering the inner beauty of others and then releasing the outer beauty.

Sherlisa Walker
Co-Author

Sherlisa Diamond Walker was born and raised in Waco, Texas and currently resides in Little Rock, Arkansas along with her three children and fiancé. She is the owner and operator of Salon Royale' Beauty and nail bar. She is a licensed cosmetologist, certified lash technician, advanced nail technician, and soon to be medical nail technician with emphasis on diabetic and fungal foot and nail care.

Sherlisa spent 21 years as an award-winning retail manager working for companies such as Best Buy, Glamour Shots, and the Footlocker Inc., but did not feel she was living within her purpose until she decided to study and return to the beauty industry. She has a strong passion for developing and training other technicians within her industry and often refers back to her trainings in retail to build courses and curriculum to help tailor her unique teaching style.

In addition, along with her children she has added a successful Royalty' themed t-shirt line to her business through *Diamond Girl Cosmetics,* which is the apparel and accessory side of her beauty/barber brand. Their mission is to deliver great products and services to clients and customers affording them the opportunity to feel like Royalty' whenever they connect with the brand.

As for writing, Sherlisa has always used it as a tool to heal and express herself through her works. Although *Depressed Yet Not Defeated* is her first published literary work, it will surely take you on a thrilling and suspenseful ride addressing many obstacles that couples and artistic individuals alike face today. Faced with the realization of infidelity and betrayal, eventually the stories main character Diamond must take a deep look within in order to understand where things could have gone wrong. Will she and her lover be able to work out their differences or will they crumble and fall? Only time will tell if their love can sustain and Reign Supreme...

Requests for t-shirt orders can be sent to diamondgirlcosmetics5@gmail.com.

~The End~